They Came to Hunt

Recolle
of a
Whitetail Guide

Best wishes,
Jack Skille

by

Jack M. Skille

Copyright © 2003
Turnbow Publishing
1114 Bear Creek Road
Princeton, Idaho 83857
(208) 875-1248

ISBN: 0-9744873-0-9

Printed in the United States of America by
Maverick Publications, Inc. • Bend, Oregon

To my father, Mike Skille, who instilled in
me his love for hunting.

Contents

Preface

I would like to tell you that I had some well thought out plan for writing this book, but I didn't. I did, however, have a lot of things to say about many subjects related to whitetail hunting and guiding. As a long-time whitetail guide, I had drawn conclusions about hunting methods, rifles, and gear, and I had what I thought were some entertaining and informative stories. Without a grand scheme, the book took its own direction and became part autobiography, part hunting stories, and part how-to for whitetail hunting. Consequently, each chapter stands alone and the book can be read in any order.

The autobiography sections will give you an insight into how and why I got into the guiding business. The earliest recollections are of my boyhood in Wisconsin, where I killed my first deer with Uncle Frank's old .32 Remington. The later years center around outfitting and guiding in Idaho. This book contains much about my father because he strongly influenced my decision to become a guide. I learned a lot of what I know about people, whitetail hunting, and gun handling from him.

This is not a work of fiction. The guiding stories are true, although some may seem unbelievable. I wrote them to entertain but to also give readers a feel for the good and bad experiences I had as a guide dealing with dozens of hunters from all over the country—strangers who became my hunting partners for a week.

The how-to parts are here for a couple of reasons. First, all those days afield with hunters gave me a chance to observe what works and what doesn't. I formed some opinions—my wife would say strong opinions—about hunting and have passed those on in these chapters.

Also, I have a problem with many of the hunting stories that I read in magazines and books or see on videos these days. Many of them are factual, entertaining, and helpful for hunters, but sadly, many are not true and are misleading, especially to those new to the sport. I know, because I have guided some of those misled hunters. So, it is my hope that these chapters will give you more of an honest, straightforward look at whitetail hunting.

You will find something entertaining, get some new ideas, and maybe even be provoked to think differently about the way you hunt whitetails. As I used to tell my hunters, "I can't guarantee you will get what you came for, only that you will have a good time on the hunt."

While reading, you may, at times, get the feeling that guiding has made me cynical. Dealing with the public can do that to a person but I hope I have only been slightly affected. Over all, I loved those years and I cherish the memories and friendships they produced. If I could take each of you with me on a whitetail hunt in this beautiful state, I would. However, the closest we can get is to imagine being out there together chasing those big Idaho bucks. Let's get after them!

Jack Skille
Princeton, Idaho

Introduction

As hunters, we dream of that once-in-a-lifetime whitetail hunt with an honest and knowledgeable guide in some distant land of big bucks. A dream hunt that starts each morning with the smell of coffee and a wonderful breakfast that we didn't have to make. Where the planning, scouting, treestand hanging, and ground blinds have all been taken care of. Where an experienced guide is at our side to help us enjoy exciting days of fair chase in beautiful wild surroundings. Where the evenings find us sitting around the fire sharing a drink and the day's hunting stories with good company. The dream builds to the moment when the guide whispers, "There's a dandy!" and ends with us doing everything right and coming home with a great trophy and memories of an adventure that we can relive for a lifetime.

I can tell you from experience that Jack Skille knows how to make dreams come true for whitetail hunters. From 1985 until 1998 dozens of fortunate hunters booked whitetail hunts with *Idaho Whitetail Guides* where they were treated to some of the finest whitetail hunting found anywhere—stories of many of those great hunts are told in these chapters. *They Came to Hunt* is full of excellent tips on how to hire a guide, what to expect on a guided hunt, equipment to bring, and mistakes to avoid. It should be required reading for any hunter contemplating booking a guided hunt. This wealth of information about guided hunts and whitetail hunting is presented in stories with wonderful style and subtle humor. I wish all of you could have experienced a hunt with Jack—your whitetail dreams would have ended well.

This book had to be written. As long as I have known Jack Skille, he has had a book in his head just waiting to be told. His love of the outdoors, wild things, and hunting are reflected in this work. Jack's respect and concern for his hunters come through in his acceptance of their abilities, no matter how limited. He uses each hunting story to teach a lesson, provide an example, or to show how things can go wrong or even become dangerous. At the same time, his stories provide insight into what it takes to turn that once-in-a-lifetime opportunity into the buck of your dreams.

Jack and I first met in graduate school at the University of Idaho, in 1972. He was working his way west from Wisconsin and I was moving north from my home state of Colorado. Idaho gave us both the opportunities to further our education and at the same time put us in the heart of some of the best elk, deer and bear hunting in the Lower 48. We were teamed on a research project and immediately discovered our shared love of the outdoors and hunting. For the past 31 years we have remained close and have shared many outdoor adventures. He has taught me everything I know about whitetail hunting.

I consider Jack my closest friend. He lifts my spirit and always makes me laugh. His book has not disappointed me on either score. I hope you will enjoy this book as much as I have. You will learn some things about whitetail hunting and guiding and most importantly, how to realize that dream hunt.

Rick Stowell

"Jack told me to stand here and be ready. He left and within 20 minutes out ran this big buck. I shot it and here came Jack with that 'I told you so' smile. This was the start of Jack's whitetail guiding and my whitetail hunting." Rick Stowell.

CHAPTER 1

Coming by it Honestly

You might say I was born into the world of guiding. My father, Marvin Skille — Mike to all who knew him — had been guiding musky fishermen in northern Wisconsin long before I was born in 1947. Our family had a small dairy farm near Stone Lake, a town about 25 miles south of Hayward, known today as the Musky Capital of the World. Most farmers during the years before WWII had to have a second source of income to make it. Dad had two, trapping in the winters and guiding in the summers.

In the 1930s and '40s, guiding fishermen was tough physical work. It amounted to rowing a 16-foot cedar-strip boat for 10-12 hours a day while the clients cast or trolled big spoons and bucktails. Outboard motors were almost unheard of, and my dad would row from the middle seat while two fishermen, one in the bow and one in the stern, would flail the lures. Back then, fishermen were primarily after trophy muskies, many of which would weigh 25-45 pounds.

My father's routine during the summer guiding season started when he rose about 4:30 each morning and milked 20-25 head of Guernsey cows by himself. We lived in a big farmhouse and while Dad was in the barn, my mother Alta would get breakfast started and wake the fishermen staying in our upstairs bedrooms. By the time the milking was done and my dad was back in the house, everyone would be up and ready to eat. After breakfast, I would watch Dad and the fishermen load their gear into our old, blue Chevy pickup and head for one of the local musky lakes.

Most of Dad's clients in those days were from Chicago and they traveled to northern Wisconsin by passenger train. One of my most vivid memories is of waiting with Dad at the Soo Line Railroad Station in Stone Lake for the train to arrive with the fishermen. I can still feel the excitement of seeing that big black train coming around the bend and along the east shore of Stone Lake.

Those fishermen were city folks and a different breed from what I was used to seeing around Stone Lake. They wore pressed trousers and white shirts; some had neckties, and most wore brown leather jackets, felt hats, and polished shoes. They contrasted sharply with the local guides who were there to pick them up. Most of the guides made their livings farming or logging and like my dad, dressed in working man's clothing.

The fishermen smelled of cigar and pipe smoke, brandy, and cologne. Dad and the other guides smelled of chewing tobacco, cow barns, and sweat. Although those fishermen were educated and obviously flush with money, they always seemed a little in awe of those weathered and hardened northern woodsmen.

I marveled at the equipment those big-city fishermen brought with them. Most had leather suit cases, metal rod cases with screw-on caps, and big, gray tackle boxes with labels like South Bend or Falls City. Their gear was great stuff to the eyes of a northwoods boy.

The musky casting outfits of these men were the very best for that time. Reels were Pflueger Supremes, Summits, and Akrons and they were mounted on rods made of solid steel or fiberglass. The more discriminating fishermen arrived with light, hollow rods of beryllium copper and reels with handles of ivory.

My brother Dennis, who is 12 years older than I am, started guiding when he was about 16 and continued for many years. Unlike our dad, who worked for himself and had a well-established reputation and repeat clients, my brother guided for lodges or resorts in the area. In the 1950s and '60s, lodges on the good fishing lakes catered to men who would come without families and were there to fish with their friends.

Dennis and other young local men like him were paid by the lodges, which arranged fishing trips, supplied boats, and provided lunches for guides and clients. It was a better arrangement for the guides, and with the increasing popularity of outboard motors, guiding became somewhat easier. As a guide for the lodges, my brother was often asked to guide for walleye, bass, and panfish. The pure trophy musky fishermen were less common than in the days when Dad started guiding.

My folks had sold their farm in 1960 and bought a resort on Lake Sissabagama, south of Stone Lake. By then the lodges in the area were calling themselves resorts and renting furnished cabins to families. Dennis had moved on to jobs that were more steady than guiding. The days of the fishing lodges were fading and family resorts were becoming popular. Occasionally, fishermen staying at our resort or others nearby would contact me asking for a guide.

I guided my first fishermen in the summer of 1961, when I was 14 years old. It was exciting, fun, and a way to make more money than mowing lawns like other kids. It was also a great learning experience, and though I didn't realize it at the time, was my initiation into what lay ahead.

As a kid with no experience, I'm sure being "Mike's boy" got me those early guiding jobs. He had a well-established name as an exceptional guide and, more importantly, a good and honest fellow. I felt a big responsibility to uphold my father's reputation.

That first guiding job was for a father and his son, who was about my age. As I recall, I guided them for three days and got paid $20 per day, which was the going rate at that time for a guide my age. Sixty dollars was more money than I could have made in a week working for local farmers or mowing lawns at resorts.

We fished for bass and crappie during the day and walleye in the evening. I knew the lake well and we were reasonably successful. I was able to share the fishing tricks I had learned and got them into some good fishing. This father and son pair caught several 2-4 pound walleye plus a couple of dozen crappie and bass each day. For a young, backwoods teenager, it was an unbelievable feeling of pride to have people, especially adults, depending on me.

In about 1960 my father started guiding hunters. My folks were renting their resort cabins to deer hunters during the November whitetail seasons, and many of them were new to the area and knew little about how or where to hunt. Dad had no trouble making the transition from fishing guide to hunting guide.

Putting on deer drives was the most successful method Dad used to guide deer hunters. He had permission to make drives on much of the private land in the area. Stillhunting was not feasible since it was limited to hunters who really knew the woods. Many of the hunting concepts we now take for granted, such as using scents, patterning, rattling and calling had not been "invented" yet. Baiting and treestand hunting were illegal for rifle hunters back then, so driving deer was Dad's only option.

Organizing drives with a bunch of green hunters was difficult and required a lot of legwork from my dad. He would hike 3-4 hunters into an area and line them up where he thought the deer would come through. Then he would take the rest of the party around to the start of the drive, line them up, and at a predetermined time, or using a shout to get them started, the drivers would push deer through to the standers.

Deer drives could be anywhere from several hundred yards to over a mile in length and several could be made in a long day. It was very common for drivers to get turned around or for standers to wander off. Dad would have to run them down before they got themselves hopelessly lost in the big woods of northern Wisconsin.

The hunters were tired by the end of each day and it was exhausting work for a guide. However, Dad was a tough, lean man who could hike all day even though he was then in his late 50s. As a trapper and hound hunter during much of the winter months, he was used to hiking many miles in a day, often on snowshoes. There were few men who could match his stamina.

I helped with some of Dad's deer guiding, since I knew many of the areas and drives. It was a great experience to be a part of planning the drives and watching the excitement of the hunters, many of whom were on their first deer hunt in northern

Wisconsin. I loved sitting around the wood stoves in the cabins hearing the stories at the end of each day's hunt. Even then, I thought guiding was more fun than just hunting.

Growing up in that setting taught me much about dealing with people in general and sportsmen in particular. I quickly realized that sportmen have different reasons for fishing and hunting and a wide range of sporting ethics. Most are good and generous people who are fun to be with, while a few are competitive, demanding bores. I had no idea at the time, but those experiences were valuable lessons that would help me as a guide 25 years later. Even though I was just a kid, I had gotten hooked on those things that have kept guides in the business—having others look to them for direction, sharing what they know about the sport, and being in charge. I have been hooked ever since.

I continued to guide deer hunters with Dad until I finished high school in 1965. With a love for hunting, fishing and everything outdoors, it was natural for me to go on to college in the field of biology. In 1969 I graduated from the University of Wisconsin at Stevens Point, which is located in the central part of Wisconsin. Then I went on to school in South Dakota where, in 1971, I received a master of science degree in wildlife biology.

That same year I married Carolyn Stoehr, whom I had met back in Stevens Point a couple of years earlier. Carolyn was raised in a hunting and fishing family and we had a mutual love for anything outdoors. Little did she know back in the early 1970s where this gangly Norwegian she married, plus her love for the outdoors, would take her.

I went to work for the Wisconsin Department of Natural Resources (DNR) the same spring Carolyn and I married. We moved to Spooner, the DNR headquarters for the Northwestern Region of Wisconsin and the town I was born in 25 years earlier. My job was working on a fisheries research project on the Chippewa Flowage, a world famous trophy musky reservoir. After that first summer of fieldwork, I found myself in the office for the winter analyzing data and writing reports. Carolyn was teaching school and we were starting to settle into married life and our careers.

However, I soon began to get an itch to move on to something different. I wanted to see the West. I had always dreamed of living out west, packing into the mountains on horses and hunting elk, mule deer, mountain goats, and sheep.

I read everything I could find about hunting out west. One of my favorite authors was Jack O'Connor, who wrote about hunting in Wyoming for antelope, Colorado for mule deer, Montana for sheep, and Idaho for elk. I wanted to get to one of those states and I knew that one possible way was to go back to school.

With Carolyn's help, I wrote to dozens of schools in about six western states to see if there were any graduate programs open for someone with my background. The plan was for me to return to school and continue my education, but I knew that my passion for hunting was pulling us west.

In the spring of 1972 I was accepted into the University of Idaho at Moscow. Moscow was situated in the heart of Idaho's great elk country, and was only a few hours from good mule deer, antelope, bighorn sheep, black bear, and mountain goat hunting. Though I had no idea when we moved there, I was soon to learn that the Panhandle of northern Idaho contained some of the best whitetail hunting anywhere in the country. To top it off, Moscow was only 30 miles north of Lewiston where my lifelong idol, Jack O'Connor, was still living and writing. I remember telling Carolyn, "If Jack O'Connor chose to live in this part of the West, it has to be right for us."

Carolyn and I soon settled into our new state. She taught elementary school in the small town of Potlatch just north of Moscow. I started graduate classes and a research project.

Every weekend we would camp, hike, and explore this new world of ours in Idaho. We started seeing elk in the higher country east of Moscow. We had never observed elk in the wild before and we both marveled at how fast and quietly they could move out of sight in spite of their tremendous size. That first summer we took several hiking trips into the Clearwater Mountain range where we saw more black bear than we had seen in all of our years in Wisconsin. In the more open high country we encountered mule deer and occasionally saw mountain goats on the rocky peaks.

Our greatest surprise, however, was the numbers and sizes of whitetail deer in the low elevation areas adjacent to the farm- lands along the western edge of Idaho. I could not recall ever reading about whitetail in Idaho and, in fact, had no idea they were even in the state. Nevertheless, here they were and in habi- tat not all that much different from where I had hunted them back home.

During the summer months leading up to the September 15 opening date of big game season I made hunting plans with my newfound college buddies. Many of these guys were from the West and they were mostly interested in elk and mule deer hunt- ing. So, during those first few hunting seasons in Idaho I spent my spare time from September until early November hunting elk in the low mountains east of Moscow and mule deer to the south in the open, arid Snake River country. We would hunt black bear in the spring when they were out on open hillsides feeding on new grass and young plants.

One year I drew a mountain goat permit in the Kelly Creek drainage of the Clearwater Region and hunted in those high, rocky peaks that were different from anything I had ever expe- rienced. I hunted alone for several days in a very remote area and spent hours stalking and climbing. The goat I shot was only of modest size but to me it was the hunt of a lifetime.

I was starting to get the hang of western hunting. I sold my old Winchester Model 100 autoloader in .308 Winchester and replaced it with a bolt action Ruger Model 77 in 7-mm. Remington Magnum caliber, complete with scope and sling. Bolt actions were traditional for the West, scopes were a great ad- vantage in the open country, and all of my western hunting bud- dies had slings. The combination was part of western hunting. This was the first bolt action rifle, scope, and sling ever owned by anyone in my family. As I was growing up, Dad's well-worn statement about bolt action rifles pretty much summed up the average Wisconsin hunter's opinion of them.

He would wrinkle up his face like he was sucking on a lemon and say, "They might be okay for the military, but too clumsy and slow for deer hunting."

His opinion of scopes was even more to the point, "They can't be trusted. They'll fog up and get bumped out of line."

As for slings, they weren't needed back home in the thick cover, where we hunted deer like we were walking-up quail, ready for a "flush" at any moment.

I remember feeling a little guilty about getting rid of my Wisconsin deer rifle and didn't tell anyone back home for several months. I really took to the new rifle set-up and started making shots at distances I had never imagined when I was growing up back home.

During my first few years in Idaho I killed a 6X6 bull elk, a good 4X4 mule deer buck, a black bear over 400 pounds, and a mountain goat. I loved hunting the big game animals in the mountains but I was always being pulled to the whitetail hunting in the lower elevations. I was like a bird dog pup that got his start on quail—I got my start on whitetail as a kid and could never be weaned off them.

Each fall, when most of my friends had put away their rifles after elk season and concluded that big game season was all but over, I hunted whitetails. I had grown up with a 9-day deer season in Wisconsin and now I was overwhelmed by the chance to hunt bucks through the entire month of November.

I was also surprised at how few hunters were after whitetail. It was a common attitude for many Idaho hunters to only kill whitetail bucks if they happened upon one while elk hunting. Consequently, Idaho whitetail season opened without much fanfare. This was a big contrast to opening day back home. There, the season always started with a scramble of hunting vehicles and a mad-house of hunters in blaze-orange making drives, shooting and shouting.

Idaho still had some of the old Wild West flavor. Hunters were not required to wear red and could legally have loaded and uncased guns in their vehicles. I would rarely see hunters actually hunting in the woods. Most local folks would drive the roads, often with Mom and the kids or a couple of buddies, and look for an easy deer to kill from the rig. To me, Idaho was a whitetail hunter's paradise and it seemed like trophy bucks were plentiful for anyone willing to get into the woods after them.

The author killed this Idaho buck in 1974. It was the first time he had hunted where he could pass up small bucks and wait for a big one.

In 1974, I killed my first Idaho whitetail, which scored 153 Boone and Crockett (B&C) points. It was the first time in my life that I had actually passed up bucks waiting for a big one, something almost unheard of back home. Idaho had vast areas of federal, state, and timber company lands wide-open to hunting and practically no one was hunting.

Over the next few years I began to hunt more for big whitetail bucks. Elk hunting took a back seat and became just a way to fill our freezer. I usually planned at least one annual pack-in hunt for mule deer, black bear or goats, but I lived for the November whitetail hunts.

In 1977 I finished graduate school in wildlife science and took a job at the University of Idaho. I was the first in our family to go on to college, let alone graduate school. My dad often joked that I went to graduate school longer than he went to school. This was true, since he only finished the sixth grade, but I would remind him that he still knew more than I did. When it came to hunting and guiding, he really did.

Carolyn continued teaching and we moved to 10 acres in the country near Princeton, Idaho. I had learned enough carpentry skills from summer jobs on house construction crews in Wisconsin to be able to start building our own house. With help from friends, we finished it in the early 1980s.

Several Wisconsin friends had been hinting about traveling west on hunting trips. With a place in the country and more free time, now that I was out of school, I started inviting them to join me on hunts each fall. I put together several hunts into the mountains for elk, mule deer, and bear and we had some great times on those trips.

For those friends who were more interested in whitetail hunting, we would stay at our home in the country and hunt from there. Of course, I wasn't a licensed outfitter or guide and didn't charge anyone for those hunts, but the old love for guiding that I had felt way back on Lake Sissabagama over 20 years earlier was starting to rekindle.

While hunting with others, I often found myself organizing the group and planning the hunts. I was usually the one crouched over a bare place on the ground, drawing in the dirt with a stick, and saying "Hey, guys, I've got an idea how we could hunt this area." I think my early days of hearing my dad and brother talk about their guiding, my experiences guiding fishermen, along with some natural tendencies to organize, all added up to my being destined to guide big game hunters.

In 1985 I made a decision to pursue an outfitter's license in Idaho and to guide for whitetail deer. At that time there were very few parts of Idaho not tied up under existing licenses. Many outfitters worked areas that were established decades ago by their forefathers and were passed down through the generations.

The area where I wanted to guide had great whitetail deer hunting but had been overlooked for its guiding potential. Up until that time, whitetail were not considered by the outfitting community as a viable species to attract hunters. I remember being told by veteran outfitters that I would never get eastern hunters to come to Idaho to hunt whitetail deer. Their reasoning was that the East was known for its whitetail hunting and there was little reason for those hunters to travel to Idaho when they could hunt whitetail at home.

Ignoring their pessimism, I went ahead with the application process to become a licensed outfitter and guide for whitetail. Carolyn and I had a home base where we could house and feed hunters. We staked out a 460 square mile area that had not been guided before. This area contained some of the best deer hunting in North America, and we both had the enthusiasm that comes from being young, ambitious, and a little naive.

In the spring of 1985 we received our license — after 20 years, I was officially back into guiding. We began advertising and by that fall *Idaho Whitetail Guides* was up and running. With Idaho's great whitetail hunting potential, we had no trouble catching the interest of hunters from across the country and for the next 14 years they came to hunt!

CHAPTER 2

Rifles for Big Deer

A book on whitetail guiding would not be complete with
out some discussion of rifles. I have spent as much time
as anyone pondering the question of what makes the
perfect rifle, scope, and caliber combination for whitetail. I love
the subject. I have dog-eared the pages in my old hunting books
that discuss guns for deer.

In addition, I'm a sucker for buying any hunting magazine
that features articles such as "The Best Rifle for Whitetail," "The
Perfect Deer Caliber," or "Carmichel on Scopes for Whitetail."
We can learn a lot from these writings but it's easy to become
confused and even exasperated over the subject. I am not going
to add to the confusion here by going into detail about the pros
and cons of various rifles and calibers, but I have got to give
you my thoughts for fear of bursting if I don't.

I will be the first to admit that I have not seen all and done
all when it comes to rifles, bullets, cartridges, and scopes. I have
never done a controlled test on the subject and none of my theo-
ries are based on science, which puts me in the same league as
most gun writers. My opinions are subjective and based on what
I have seen and experienced.

However, while guiding I was fortunate to have had the opportunity to see many rifles and cartridges used to kill (or attempt to kill) deer—many more deer than what I could have
killed in several lifetimes of hunting. I have seen them shot with
everything from the diminutive .22 Hornet (my wife's first buck)
to the potent .338 Winchester Magnum. As you might expect, I

also field dressed most of the bucks killed by my hunters and was able to see bullet performance up close and personal. All of this experience has given me some opinions on the suitability of various rifles and cartridges for whitetail.

Through most of my guiding years, I kept a record of the rifle makes, models, calibers, and scopes used by my hunters. It is no surprise that 83 percent carried bolt actions, far out numbering other actions. I did see pump actions, semiautomatics, and lever actions (in that order) but very few. A total of eight of my hunters showed up with semiautomatics and they were from the states of Wisconsin, Pennsylvania, Vermont, and Massachusetts. Autoloaders and slide actions have always been more popular in that part of the country than out west. The reason must lie somewhere with the notion that bolt actions were best suited for the deliberate long range shooting in the West where accuracy was more important than speed. Conversely, pumps and autoloaders provided the fast follow-up shots thought to be needed in the thick cover east of the Mississippi River. One exception has been the popularity of the lever actions in the western states explained by their ease in being carried in saddle scabbards.

I have a story dealing with pump action and autoloading rifles and Mid-western hunters that I just have to tell — bear with me while I diverge here for a bit. One fall I booked Pat and Mark, two young hunters from Wisconsin who had never been out west and had never hunted any big game other than deer in Wisconsin. When they showed up they spent a little time the first day shooting their rifles to make sure all was well. I always had a shooting bench and target set up at camp so hunters could easily check their rifles and scopes.

Their rifles were Remingtons; one was a Model 742 BDL semiautomatic carbine in .30-'06 and the other was a Model 760 BDL pump action in .308 Winchester. Both rifles were equipped with the type of scope mounts that make it possible to look under the scope and use the iron sights. These "see-through" mounts, as they have been called, were popular in the days when scopes were new to the hunting world and scope accuracy was not trusted. However, on most rifles they force the hunter to hold his head so high to see through the scope that only his chin touches the stock. In fact, on some rifles the scope is so high that a shooter can not rest any part of his face on the stock. Generally, they make for a very unwieldy and wobbly set-up for accurate shooting with a scope.

These young fellows each took three or four shots at 100 yards. They only shot about 5 or 6-inch groups, pretty dismal for scope sighted rifles but they seemed to be happy and said they were ready to hunt. I had expected them to do better since shooting from a bench should have eased the problems caused by those high mounted scopes. I didn't interfere since they indicated that was how the guns were shooting when they left home. One thing I've learned over the years is that every hunter has his own idea of acceptable accuracy and I wasn't about to discourage these boys by being critical of their shooting.

A couple of days later, Mark killed a respectable 10-point buck with a pretty drop-point on one side. He made a good shot but the buck was standing and only about 60 yards away. That evening at the dinner table as he was re-telling the story to the other hunters in camp he got into more detail about the shot he made that day.

He described how the buck stepped out, how he eased the rifle to his shoulder, quickly got the buck in his scope, and dropped his eye down to the iron sights and shot. Well, the rest of us at the table were all dumbfounded. Someone asked Mark why he bothered carrying a scope at all if he always shot using the iron sights. He explained that he used the scope to get a better look at the deer but never trusted it for the actual shot. Pat used the same logic and they explained that everyone in their hunting gang back in Wisconsin supported this line of thinking.

Of course, that explained why their shooting from a bench rest at 100 yards was not impressive. They had both been shooting with iron sights which I was not aware of.

My point in telling this story is two-fold. First, if you were to check around the country you would find a fairly wide range

A Wisconsin hunter (left) and guide, Donny Ball. This hunter used a .30-'06 Remington Model 742 carbine with a scope on see-through mounts, a combination not seen much among western hunters.

of opinions about what rifle and scope set-up is best for white-tails. Secondly, I have learned not to be too critical of someone else's rifle and its accessories. What I might think is a miserable set-up for me may work just fine for another hunter.

Let us get back to the statistics I collected from my hunters over the years. As for make of rifle, Remingtons were the most popular among my hunters. The Remington Model 700 BDL made up about 30 percent of rifles carried. Ruger, Browning, and Winchester followed in this order. About 10 percent of my clients came with custom-made rifles made up on various actions.

Over 95 percent of my hunters used variable power scopes and the 2X-7X was the most popular. Sixty-six percent had rifles topped with Leupold brand scopes. Only one hunter used a rifle with open sights—a Model 94 Winchester in .30-30 caliber.

The top five cartridges used were the .270 Winchester (31%), .30-'06 (22%), .308 Winchester (10%), .243 Winchester and .300 Winchester Magnum (each at 9%). Among all my hunters, eighteen different cartridges were used ranging from the .30-30 and .243 Winchesters up through the .300 Weatherby and .338 Winchester Magnums.

Therefore, if one were to put together a rifle based on the data I collected from my hunters it would be a bolt action Remington Model 700 BDL with a 22-inch barrel, weighing about 7 pounds. It would be a long action chambered for the .270 Winchester. The scope would be a Leupold 2X-7X variable, and the rifle would carry a sling about 90 percent of the time and some kind of scope covers about 98 percent of the time. This set-up is about as middle-of-the-road as a rifle can be. It could be used for most game in North America including whitetail anywhere they live.

The bulk of my whitetail hunting and guiding has been here in northern Idaho, where shots at bucks are usually in heavy timber and at close-range. Open country broadside shots at standing, unaware deer have been the exception. Stillhunting was usually through thick brush where it was tough to be quiet and stealthy. Often, shots were at running deer or deer that presented odd angles and partial views. Many of my hunters shot deer from treestands where they had to hoist their rifles up by rope or slung on their backs. Treestand platforms did not allow much room for maneuvering.

These conditions called for rifles with particular attributes. Hunters with light, short barreled, fast handling rifles seemed to do best. With these rifles they could get through the timber and brush easier and with less noise. They could get them to the shoulder faster and on target quicker for running shots or shots at deer about to bolt. Moreover, they were much handier for treestand hunting.

Rifles like the Remington Model Seven, the Ruger Model 77 Ultra Light and Ultra Light Carbine, and Winchester's Featherweights and Lightweights really fit the bill for this kind of hunting. Their 22-inch or shorter barrels (some as short as 18 ½ inches), weights of around six pounds, and short overall lengths made them ideal. As a guide, I advocated these rifles every time hunters asked for my opinion.

Bucks like this one that field dressed 221 pounds, take some killing. The hunter used a .300 Winchester Magnum, which the author feels is not overkill.

Though smaller was better for rifles under these hunting conditions, that did not prove to be the case for whitetail cartridges. Cartridges and bullets that had enough energy and weight to put deer down fast were the logical choices for our hunting. The heavy timber made second shots rare and tracking difficult. Hunters were paying big money for hunts-of-a-lifetime and could not afford to lose deer. It may sound self-seeking, but I had a reputation at stake and lost bucks did nothing for my guiding business. These Idaho bucks were big animals, often field dressing over 200 pounds (that is 250 pounds live weight) and bucks of that size take some killing.

I gradually concluded that cartridges in the .243 and 6-mm. category were too small. I have heard the hype about high velocity and its great killing effect, but I have not witnessed it. There is no question that light, fast bullets will kill deer, but my experience has been that they do not put big bucks down quickly.

I have seen a few large bucks hit solidly with bullets from those mild cartridges, yet show little or no reaction although they died quickly. With more potent cartridges pushing heavier bullets, big deer generally show some sign of being hit and do not travel as far, if at all. The smallest cartridges I felt comfortable with were those in the .308, .270. and .30-'06 range.

Just how serious did I think this light cartridge problem was? Well, if you had shown up at my hunting camp with a .243 Winchester, 6-mm. Remington, or even one of the .22 caliber high velocity center fires I would not have run you off. Incidently, any centerfire cartridge is legal for hunting deer in Idaho. I would, however, have kept your cartridge choice in the back of my mind as we hunted. I would not have said, "take him" on a going away shot, a head-on shot, or a running shot through heavy timber. If the rifle were one you had used a lot and you seemed to be a confident and deliberate shot, I would not have been too concerned.

On the other hand, if you had shown up with something like a .338 Winchester Magnum or bigger, would I have fainted away? Not at all, if you could shoot it well. The big belted magnums would be fine for whitetail except they require big heavy rifles to keep them from kicking the daylights out of the average hunter. Most hunters would rather carry lighter weight rifles, which usually precludes the magnum cartridges.

I do not buy the idea that big guns are "overkill." Most hunters these days are not concerned with meat destruction so that is less of an issue. If a hunter is built like a stevedore and can handle the recoil I say "more power to him," literally. With the big boomers a hunter should not hesitate to take a shot from any angle, including the going-away shot.

Keep in mind that my opinions about what makes a good whitetail rifle are mainly based on my experiences hunting and guiding in northern Idaho. However, I believe that a good rifle for Idaho whitetail would work well in many whitetail states. Before a hunter puts a rifle and scope combination together, he should give thought to what the conditions are where he plans to do most of his hunting. For situations requiring long shots across open fields at standing bucks a light, short-barreled rifle with big punch, topped with a low-power scope may not be the proper choice. The ideal Idaho whitetail rifle is not a set-up for whitetail where they are hunted on big fields in the South, open prairies in Canada, flat agricultural land in Kansas and the Dakotas, or the river bottom alfalfa fields of Montana. Those situations call for heavier rifles with longer barrels that hold steady for long shots — flat shooting guns with high velocity and lighter bullets. Open country hunting also requires high magnification scopes where slow, careful aiming is possible.

I have killed deer with rifles as outdated and nostalgic as a lever action Winchester Model 94 with an octagon barrel and crescent butt plate in .32 Winchester Special and a Remington Model 14 pump in .32 Remington. I have shot deer with not-so-common calibers like the 7x57 Mauser, .257 Roberts and the .35 Whelen Improved. In addition, I have shot deer with cartridges as common as 7mm-08, .308, .270, and 7-mm. Remington Magnum. I have shot deer with pumps, lever actions, autoloaders, and bolt actions.

Nevertheless, after all this flirting with different rifles and calibers, in 1980 I promised myself to a pre-'64 Winchester Model 70 Featherweight in .30-'06 as my lifelong deer rifle. This is not because the caliber is sexy and interesting — Jack O'Connor called it the "workhorse of cartridges." It is not because the rifle is anything new and improved — it was made before WWII. I have settled on it because it fits me, is lightweight, is more accurate than I am, and most importantly, I am very used to it.

This old rifle stays sighted in year after year. It is accurate with several bullet weights, although I stick with 180 grain for most of my hunting. The rifle was custom stocked for me by Lloyd Alexander of Genesee, Idaho and checkered by his wife Vera. The stock is a beautiful piece of Claro walnut with ebony inlays checkered in the classic fleur-de-lis pattern. The scope on this rifle is a variable 1¾X-5X Redfield that I mail ordered from *Gander Mountain* in 1973. It is the first scope I ever hunted with and is still in good condition. This rifle is well worn and carries the scars of many hunts — all of which make it more dear to me.

With this rifle, I have shot dozens of whitetail, several black bear and a few elk and mule deer.

If I were shopping for a new whitetail rifle to replace my old one for close range timber hunting, here is what I would look for. First, I would go for a bolt action, since they tend to be dependable, have good accuracy, generally have decent triggers, and handle scope sights well. I would be looking for a rifle not heavier than 6 ½ pounds, bare naked. It could not have a barrel longer than 22 inches; 20 inches would be better. I would take a composite stock since they are generally lighter and stronger than wood. Frankly, I have not gotten used to the looks of most of the modern composite stocks but I accept them for their practicality.

As for this new rifle having a stainless steel barrel and action, it makes little difference to me. This latest craze about stainless steel baffles me. Many hunters these days look at blued steel as though it will turn to rust and disintegrate with the first rain drop. The world has been hunting for a very long time without stainless steel and doing just fine. If a hunter is careless enough to leave his rifle in the potato cellar over winter then he definitely needs stainless steel and a composite stock. I would plan to be more careful with this new rifle.

The gun would have a short action to keep the weight down and give it a quicker bolt throw. The barrel would not need sights since I would put a scope on it. Having a short action narrows my choice of cartridges but this is no handicap with all the short cartridges to choose from these days. I like heavy bullets and would settle for nothing smaller than 30 caliber. The old dependable .308 Winchester would be fine but I would look seriously at the new short .30 caliber magnums.

On this new rifle, I would buy the best scope I could afford. It would be a variable in the 1½X-5X range, possibly 2X-7X power but not more, and I would mount it as low to the action as possible. I would only use scope covers to keep out dust during storage and carrying the rifle in a case. I have yet to see scope covers that function in all conditions and I hate fooling with them while hunting.

After I got this new rifle home, I would sight it in to hit two inches high at 100 yards. Then I would see where it hit at 50, 150, 200, and 250 yards. Most likely, it would shoot flat enough that I would not need to hold anywhere but dead on at these yards. For the type of whitetail hunting here in Idaho there is seldom a need to shoot beyond 250 yards.

I would plan to practice with this rifle until I became very familiar with it. That practice would go beyond just shooting and would include handling, cleaning, disassembly and assembly. I would carry it afield even if I were not hunting to get used to the feel of it in my hands and how it comes up for a shot.

I would have a lightweight, detachable nylon sling for this rifle but I would keep it in my coat pocket or fanny pack while hunting. Slings hang up on brush and add to the noise while hunting. In addition, we all have a tendency to get lazy and want to carry our rifles slung over our shoulders while hunting. This habit has saved a lot of deer. I can think of times when my hunters missed opportunities at bucks because their rifles were slung over their shoulders. The sling for this new rifle would only be used for carrying when I was dragging out a buck—hopefully, it would get a lot of use.

After getting these opinions off my chest, I no longer have the feeling that I may burst for holding them in. I have criticised some rifles, calibers, scopes and accessories and praised others. I have forced my ideas upon you about the perfect rifle for hunting big deer in Idaho. After all that, I feel strongly that these choices are of less importance than your familiarity with your rifle and your ability to shoot it fast and accurately. You will run into this opinion of mine more than once in these chapters—I feel it is worth repeating.

CHAPTER 3

Knowing Your Rifle

The arguments over "what makes the ideal whitetail hunting rifle?" will likely go on forever. I am glad there can be no final conclusion because I love the debate — it is one of the most interesting questions related to hunting. Of course, there is no right answer, and that's why it is so fascinating. When hunters get into discussing the subject we often find that the opinions differ based on hunting styles, regions, and family customs — the "Grandpa said it was so" syndrome.

However, aside from the pure fun of contemplating the various combinations of rifle, caliber, scope, etc., in the end the answer is of less significance than most of us want to admit. Personally, I have concluded that what is ultimately more important is gun familiarity. When the decisive moment arrives — when all the thinking and planning are behind and you have put in the hours and the miles and it is time to make the shot, you must know your rifle. You cannot be fumbling with the action, looking for the safety, messing with the scope, or jockeying your head to find the cross hairs.

The story of my first deer is a prime example of how things can go when a hunter is unfamiliar with his rifle. I was only 12 so I had an excuse for not knowing my rifle. As adults, none of us can use that excuse. For me it was an early lesson that has stuck with me to this day. I have owned many rifles since killing that first deer, but I eventually settled on one for whitetail hunting and got to know it well.

My father, Mike, and I went alone that day. I have called

him Mike since I was old enough to talk. This was not out of disrespect; I loved him dearly. It was just the name I learned instead of Dad. We usually hunted with my brother and sister and often some cousins and uncles. That day, however, it was just Mike and me. The place he picked was remote and took a long hike to reach. I had gotten to know many hunting areas and had gone along on several hunts before but this was a new location.

Before leaving me, Mike explained his plan. I was to stay on a narrow ridge between two pothole lakes where deer liked to travel. He would circle to the far end of the lakes and hunt through to me.

I can still see him as he eased out of sight to make the drive. His heavy, wool black and red plaid coat was buttoned tight and his collar was up to keep out the cold. He walked silently in the cold snow that came halfway up his rubber-bottom, leather-topped pack boots. Those boots were tall, with at least 20 hooks for laces and his black wool pants were tucked in to keep out the snow. He wore a black, wool guide's cap, the kind worn by guides these days with little laces on the front above the bill. In the crook of his left arm rested his Winchester, with its long octagon barrel and crescent-shaped butt plate. It had been his only rifle since he was 18 years old. He used it to kill dozens of deer, bear, and coyote and he carried the rifle like it was a part of him.

While Mike circled the lake on the left to hunt toward me down the ridge, all I had to do was wait. I stood in the cold with my back against a clump of basswood trees. I could see both lakes, each about 30-acres of snow covered ice. Also, I could see the timbered ridge between the lakes that sloped down toward me.

Before Mike left me, he had described in a coarse whisper and a breath of Copenhagen, "If deer come they'll be coming down that ridge right to you. They might try crossing one of the lakes — if they do, don't shoot. It's too far, they'll be running, and it's dangerous to shoot across ice. You don't know where your bullets might go."

He ended his pep talk with, "Wait 'till they're close, pick out a big doe or buck, and wait for it to stop. Then take one careful shot and make it count."

I had heard all that before, but it was reassuring and as a father he had to say it.

As I waited, I checked my old rifle to make sure it was loaded, that a cartridge was in the chamber, and that the safety was in the "safe" position. I was carrying my Uncle Frank's rifle that we had just picked up a couple days earlier. I barely knew how to load it and had only fired it twice at a paper plate tacked to a fence post behind our barn. I had hit the plate once and the fence post once.

I had borrowed the rifle because I didn't have one of my own. In those days, we didn't just go buy a new gun. It was a Remington Model 14 pump action in .32 Remington caliber. It held five cartridges in a tubular magazine and had buckhorn sights. It was big and heavy compared to the .22 I had used to hunt rabbits and squirrels, but this was deer hunting and deer hunting called for a big gun. It was an awesome rifle for a twelve-year-old.

Finally, I thought I saw a flash of brown far up the ridge. My heart started pounding as I waited. Was it a deer? Would it cross the lake where I'd never get a shot? Seconds crept by and I started to relax a little. Then there it was, a small deer running fast and blindly. It wasn't close, it wasn't a large doe or buck, and it wasn't going to stop.

I pulled the old rifle up to my shoulder and yanked the trigger — nothing happened. Then I realized I had forgotten to push the safety button. I put it to my shoulder a second time and yanked the trigger. This time it went off with a thunderous boom as the little deer darted between trees and leaped over logs. I aimed the gun and again I yanked the trigger — nothing happened. Then I realized I had to work the pump action. I was catching on but the deer was getting past me now. I kept shooting until, finally, the confused deer went down in a cloud of powdery snow. Through pure luck one of my wild shots had connected. I knew I hadn't been aiming and I knew that by all rights I should never have gotten the deer.

Nevertheless, my first deer was down and I waited. Finally, like a silent shadow slipping through the trees on the ridge, I could see Mike. He was tracking my deer. As we both met over the little deer, I could see a smile on his face and a twinkle in those blue Norwegian eyes. His look told me I must have done a good thing. It was okay to shoot this little deer. It was okay not to wait for it to stop. It was okay to shoot so many times, to miss so many times. His look said I was on my way into the world of hunting.

In 45 years since that unforgettable day of hunting with Uncle Frank's rifle, I have seen about every combination of guns, calibers, and sights imaginable and I've come to one simple conclusion. The choice of rifle plays only a minor role compared to the hunter's familiarity with it. It would have made little difference if that old borrowed gun had been a scope-sighted modern bolt action rifle in one of today's popular calibers. Not being accustomed to it, I still would have struggled to scratch down that little deer. Familiarity goes beyond knowing how to load the gun, work the bolt, and pull the trigger. It means knowing the rifle to the point where handling it is second nature, where the gun becomes a part of the hunter.

When I first saw a new client pull his gun from its case, load it, and take a couple of shots to check it out, I quickly got a feel for how the hunt was going to go. It was a bad sign if he handled it like a foreign object, had to look to find the safety, or tried to put one more cartridge in the magazine when it was full. I recall watching hunters put on their glasses to see if clockwise increased scope power. Often hunters had no idea that they could adjust their scopes to focus the cross-hairs. These were signs that they had not handled their rifles enough and forecasted that we were going to need an extra dose of luck during the week.

It's a sad reality but most of us spend much more time reading about rifles than we do using them. To most of us, "getting used to our gun" means taking it out to the shooting range a time or two before the hunting season.

There was a time, not too long ago, when hunters carried their rifles for many months during the year. My father told me that when he was a young man in the 1920s and '30s in northern Wisconsin he would start carrying his rifle in the early fall for bear hunting, then carry it through the rest of the fall for deer season and continue carrying it all winter for coyote hunting with hounds.

Wisconsin still had large expanses of mature timber. These old-growth forests were not good deer habitat and deer densities were low. The seasons were only open every other year, were often only three days long, and were limited to bucks only. A deer tag cost fifty cents if a hunter bothered to buy one. My father, like most others in the northwoods in those days, paid little attention to seasons or tags. He was interested in getting meat and always carried his "deer rifle."

Carrying, to him, didn't mean "behind the pickup seat" or "across the handlebars of his 4-wheeler." It meant in his hand or cradled in his arms. Most of his traveling was by foot—sometimes on snowshoes. His rifle was as much a part of him as the hat on his head or the can of chew in his shirt pocket. He just did not go many places without it.

Anyone using a rifle that much could not help but become familiar with it. My father's rifle was a Winchester Model 94 rifle, as opposed to a carbine, in .32 Winchester Special caliber. It carried a Lyman tang-mounted peep sight—a sight that was at the top of a post which stood behind the hammer and just in front of where your thumb comes over the top of the stock. The front sight was a thin blade with a small bead at the top, and was mounted 32 inches from the rear peep sight, giving this set-up a long sight radius.

Because he was so familiar with the rifle and shot it so often, he was a terrific shot with it. As a boy I remember one occasion when I watched him shoot deer that had been pushed to us in a deer drive. It was at dusk with very low light and I can still see those three deer running toward us on a route that would take them across the logging road we stood on. The distance was about 50 yards. Because of the poor light, Dad folded the rear sight down and aimed with only the front sight. As the deer bounded single file across the narrow road, he worked the lever without dropping it from his shoulder and fired one quick shot at each deer. The ground was snowcovered and I remember seeing the three deer lying within a few feet of each other about four jumps from the road—each shot near the heart.

As Dad said latter when I asked how he could shoot without the rear sight, "If you really know a rifle and hold it the same every time, the rear sight isn't all that important for a close running shot."

I inherited this rifle in 1991 when my father passed away at the age of 86. It now hangs in my house on a wall with my game heads. He had purchased this rifle for $19.00 in 1923, and hunted with nothing else for the next 40 years. In 1963 the riflings got so worn—.32 Specials were notorious for that—the rifle started losing accuracy and he had to give it up for a new one.

Jack Skille took a nostalgic step back in time when he used his father's 70-year-old Winchester Model 94 in .32 Special caliber to take this 4X4 Idaho whitetail.

My father replaced the old Winchester with a Remington Model 742 semiautomatic in .30-'06 caliber. He had a Williams peep sight side-mounted on the new rifle.

This combination of rifle and caliber was a big change for my father but autoloaders had become very popular in Wisconsin in that era. Everyone seemed to hunt with either a semiautomatic or a pump and Remingtons were very common.

After 40 years of familiarity with one rifle, my father never was able to get used to his new rifle although he shot several deer with it over the next 25 years. In about 1975 his eyesight started failing and he replaced the peep sight with a 4X Burris scope. This allowed him to hunt for several more years and he killed his last buck at the age of 83.

In his final few years, he confided to me that every time he shot a deer he would "Cock that blasted automatic." After the shot, he would "Lever the damn thing." He had become so familiar with the old Winchester that he was not able to make the switch to a new rifle. He was a great believer in being a one-gun-man. His advice to young hunters was always the same, "Buy one good rifle, don't stew over the make, model, or caliber, use it until it becomes a part of you, then stick with it."

Obviously, few of us live that kind of lifestyle or even have access to an area where we can carry a rifle as much as my father did. However, we can all find some way to handle our rifles even if we live in a penthouse in New York City.

If you want to gain real familiarity with a rifle, you first must decide on one rifle that you will call your whitetail rifle. Choose it as though you plan to be married to it—for life. Then start spending time with it. Hold that rifle while watching TV and practice with it by "shooting" targets on TV. If you don't like TV, then use birds in your bird feeder as make-believe targets—anything that will give you some chance to put the gun through the motions. Keep it empty, of course, but practice working the action, adjusting the scope, thumbing the safety and dry firing. Most modern rifles can be dry-fired with no problem.

When you are out in the field, practice throwing the rifle up to your shoulder and getting the sights on stumps or rocks, imagining they are big bucks. If you are uncomfortable having people see you playing this game then go alone. Practice getting into different shooting positions: standing off-hand, kneeling, sitting, prone, and resting over a log or against a tree. You will be amazed at how fast you start feeling confident in your ability to use your rifle without thinking. It will soon become an old and trusted friend like your favorite pair of hunting boots or comfortable wool coat.

Some folks might feel this sort of "playing" with a gun is a dangerous thing. I believe, however, there is nothing more dangerous than a hunter whose rifle is a stranger to him. He isn't aware of where it is pointed, isn't sure whether the safety is on or off, isn't sure how many rounds it's holding—or can hold—and isn't really sure how the thing works.

I am happy to say that the majority of my hunters were experienced deer hunters and were familiar enough with their rifles that there were few problems. Some were shooting enthusiasts and did a lot of off-season shooting, were very good shots, and were always aware of gun safety. Some were gun collectors and had many rifles to chose from.

I feel compelled to say a word here about gun collecting. I love guns and have been known to have many more than I could use or afford—according to my wife, anyway. For me, there seems to be an inverse relationship between the number of guns I own and the number of days I spend hunting. At the risk of generalizing—and possibly insulting gun nuts, my conclusion is that the more we collect the less we hunt. Although I still have more rifles than I can use, I have forced myself to hunt with just one. As a guide, I always felt relieved when a hunter showed up and said "Old Betsy" was his only rifle and he had hunted with her most of his life.

However, the occasional hunter came to hunt whose rifle was as foreign to him as a hair-dryer is to a monk. In the fall of 1992 I guided a young hunter from Pennsylvania—I will call him Jason—and I will never forget the hunt. It involved problems ranging from missing shots at bucks to serious gun safety issues that nearly ended his hunt.

Jason's problems all revolved around a lack of practice and familiarity with his gun. He told me on the phone that he had not hunted much but had killed a couple of deer back home when he was younger. He had always wanted to go on a guided hunt out west and now that he had a good job and could afford it, he felt like this was the time. Jason was 27 years old.

After I picked him up at the airport and he settled into camp, I asked Jason if he wanted to shoot his rifle to make sure it was sighted in. His response was not comforting.

He said, "Yes, that might be good. I haven't had a chance to shoot it since I just bought it for this hunt."

He opened the gun case and pulled out a shiny, new Remington Model 700 BDL in .308 Winchester. The rifle carried a new 2X-7X variable power Leupold scope. I immediately realized he had taken my advice to heart. In an earlier phone conversation, he had asked what I thought would be a good rifle, caliber, and scope combination for Idaho whitetail.

I had not gotten down to specific make and model but had said something like, "A good rifle would be a bolt action in a caliber not less than .308 Winchester. I'd recommend a variable scope with not more than 2 to 7 power."

This was a fine hunting combination but I was immediately worried that he had not had any time to get to know it. Jason had never shot from a bench rest and had a difficult time. This new rifle was completely alien to him. He had never used a bolt action so had trouble with the safety, loading the magazine, and operating the bolt.

First, we adjusted the scope's ocular lens for his eye so the cross-hairs were clear. I showed him how to load and unload the rifle and he asked me to take a couple shots. It had been bore-sighted at the gun shop where he bought the outfit and it was hitting paper at 100 yards. I adjusted the cross hairs until I was getting a 2-3 inch group about two inches high at 100 yards.

Jason shot several rounds and it was painfully obvious he wasn't going to be able to do much better than to keep them in a dinner-plate. At least they were somewhat scattered around the center.

He was getting tired of this whole sighting-in business and finally said, "That should be good enough, don't you think?"

This put me in a tough situation. There was no time to begin Basic Shooting 101 and it was too late to give him a refund and send him back home. We had to make the best of it. I started by gently letting him know that he was going to have to confine his shots at deer to less than 100 yards, preferably less than 50 yards.

Over the next three days Jason saw four bucks. While other hunters in camp were having trouble seeing any deer, Jason was a buck magnet. He could not go anywhere without seeing bucks. To everyone's surprise but mine he was not able to hit any of them. He shot at three of those bucks that were less than 100 yards and missed them cleanly. One buck was walking across a wide-open hillside and Jason shot twice off-hand at about 50 yards with no luck. Another was facing him in a logging road at less than 40 yards — clean miss. The third was tracking a doe along the edge of a clearcut at about 75 yards — another miss.

Kelly Phillips, my long-time guide, was with Jason when they saw the forth buck. The buck walked past them at 30 yards and Jason was not able to get the cross-hairs on him. Kelly said the buck was the largest 8-pointer he had ever seen — long, heavy points with thick beams. It was raining and the buck actually stopped and shook the water off like a dog, then continued walking.

Jason didn't appear to be as frustrated as Kelly and I were. He seemed to take it in stride as though that was the way hunting is supposed to go — like a video game where you just keep hunting and shooting and deer will keep showing up. Jason viewed his missing as just the normal tough-luck of the hunting game. I was getting worried that he would end up with nothing at the end of his 6-day hunt or, worse yet, wound a buck.

On the fourth day of the hunt I told Jason we were going to try rattling for a change of pace. My hope was that we could rattle a buck into very close range where Jason could not miss.

As it turned out, this presented a new set of problems. Up until now we had been sending Jason alone to stillhunt or

standhunt and we were not with him much. In a rattling sce-
nario we were together and it became immediately obvious that
Jason was as unsafe with his rifle as he had been inaccurate.

My first indication of a problem was when I saw his rifle
safety in the "fire" position. I pointed it out, assuming he had
forgotten to check it. He didn't say a thing as he clicked it into
the "safe" position. We set up and rattled with no luck. As we
started off to a new location, I saw that his safety was off again.

This time when I pointed it out Jason became a little annoyed
and said, "I keep the safety off so I can make a faster shot if we
rattle in a buck."

Without getting nasty, I told Jason that was not a good idea.
I said, "If you get in that habit you will forget it's off and go on
hunting with it off. It takes no time at all to slip that safety off
when you are shouldering the rifle to shoot."

I hoped I had made my point but continued to watch his
rifle. Sure enough, when we stopped to rattle I saw him slip the
safety off. He had his back to me, hoping I wouldn't notice. This
time I felt I had no choice but to show my exasperation with
him.

I said, "Jason, if you insist on keeping that safety off we will
end this hunt now. It is unsafe for me and unsafe for you."

That seemed to jar him into the reality of what he was doing
and he said, "I am afraid that if a buck comes I will forget to flip
the safety. I have to look for it each time and can never remember which position is safe and which is fire. I'm just not used to
this new gun."

He went on to express his frustration with missing those deer
and said that he didn't think he would be able to kill a buck on
this trip. He indicated he had shot off-hand at the bucks he
missed and the gun seemed awkward to him. He was loosing
confidence fast.

The next day I decided that our only hope was to get Jason
into a foolproof shooting situation. I knew of a creek-bottom
and strip of timber between two clearcuts where deer traveled.
We got there just at daylight and found a little spot on the hillside overlooking this stream. I spent some time getting Jason a

comfortable place to sit and put a log between two stumps for a shooting rest. He could sit on the ground with his back against a stump while resting his rifle over the log. I sat beside him so I could coach him through a shot if a buck showed up. We were about 50 yards above the creek and had a great view. Any deer moving up or down that creek would present a shot.

Jason liked this set-up and seemed to relax. Having someone beside him giving directions boosted his confidence and for the first time, I felt he was enjoying hunting.

He asked me where I thought deer might come, how fast they would come, and when he should shoot. I said they could come from anywhere but, pointing to an old skid trail off to the west, I said, "That would be a likely place for a buck to travel."

We had not sat more than two hours when I spotted a buck coming toward us down this skid trail. It was a moment when, as a guide, I felt like I was earning my pay.

I said in a whisper, "Don't make any fast moves but get your shoulder behind the rifle. Keep the gun on the log and follow him in your scope."

The buck reached the creek and started walking upstream to our right. He was on the far side of the creek in the trees but there were plenty of openings for a shot.

I kept whispering in Jason's ear, "Relax, take your time, don't shoot until he is broad-side directly across the creek from us."

Just as the 10-pointer crossed an opening directly below us he stopped, put his head down, and started drinking from the creek.

I whispered, "Now!" in Jason's ear.

I saw him slip off the safety and start the trigger squeeze. The .308 boomed and I could see the buck hunch. He made two or three feeble jumps and went down. The bullet had hit him just behind the front shoulder — a perfect shot.

We were both overjoyed. Jason was beginning to feel a little accustomed to his new rifle. He told me this was his first buck of any size. I was happy to see a hunt change from almost falling apart to finally having a successful ending.

For me, it reinforced my father's advice from two generations ago when he said, "Get one good rifle, don't stew over the make, model, or caliber, use it until it becomes a part of you, and then stick with it."

Jason had one good rifle and after this unforgettable hunt it was becoming a part of him. I knew he would stick with it.

*A very happy hunter with a medium-sized 10-pointer,
the largest he had ever killed.*

CHAPTER 4

They Made Guiding Easy

When outfitters or guides get together, they love to talk "guide talk." Guide talk usually means a lot of stories about the hunters who screwed up, the mistakes that were made, and all the reasons lousy hunters don't get their bucks. Negative guide talk is just an understandable aspect of human nature—like waitresses comparing notes about cheapskate customers or traffic cops describing the drunkest drivers they ever arrested—it's expected.

I have a few books in my hunting library written by guides. The same goes for these—they are full of guide talk. For some reason, the stories where "things went wrong" seem to be the first that go down on paper. That is unfortunate since some of the most interesting stories are about hunts where everything went right. We can learn things from these that we couldn't learn from the "guide talk" stories. The truth is that the majority of hunts go well, most of the hunters are great guys, and the hunts that turn sour are few and far between.

I was fortunate to be able to guide many good hunters over the years; a couple stand out in my mind as being great hunters. When I say "great hunters" I don't mean they had exceptional skills, were crack-shots, or were more woods-wise than the rest. They were experienced and capable hunters but more importantly from a guide's viewpoint, they were enjoyable to be with, took directions willingly, and were just plain easy to guide.

It Took Five Years

The first of these memorable hunters was Roy, a traveling pharmaceutical salesman from Green Bay, Wisconsin. Roy was in his 40s when he started coming to hunt with us. One might easily conjure up a picture of an out-of-shape middle aged guy who would need to be coddled. However, that was far form the case. Roy kept himself in great shape because he loved to hunt. He worked out in a gym several times a week and could climb Idaho hills easier than most people walk through their local malls.

Roy was also a dyed-in-the-wool whitetail hunter. In Wisconsin, he had hunted with rifle, bow, and shotgun since he was old enough to get a license. Roy knew whitetails and he knew how to hunt but he had never killed a big buck. He had done most of his hunting in Wisconsin and Upper Michigan where most bucks are harvested long before they are mature enough to produce trophy antlers.

Roy's first hunt with me for whitetails was in 1989 and he returned five more times. It was obvious from the start that Roy would be easy to guide. His questions were intelligent, his expectations were realistic, and he showed the patience it takes to keep coming back to try for a big buck. He did not expect it to be easy. And he did keep coming back until 1997 when he got what he was after—a good trophy Idaho buck.

Roy was a guy who liked to learn one area and not jump around to new hunting grounds. He was able to recognize buck sign and when he found it, he was like a coon hound on a fresh track—he stuck with it. His favorite place to hunt in my guiding area was the upper end of a drainage we called Olevan. It was not hunted much because it was not an easy place to get into or an easy place to hunt. The nearest road was at the bottom of the drainage and getting into the head of the watershed required a two mile up-hill hike through timber. Roy used a different route that required more hiking but was much easier. He would hike in on a long, high ridge that put him at the head of Olevan. This route was a mile longer but was relatively level and on a good trail.

Roy was the type who liked to hunt alone and did not really need a guide once he became familiar with an area. After the first year when I took him in on that ridge trail and gave him a general feel for the Olevan drainage he was confident with it. All I had to do was drop him off at the trailhead with his lunch and rifle. I could go elsewhere with other hunters for the day and pick him up after dark. I guided very few hunters who felt self-assured enough to do that.

By 1995 Roy had killed three bucks in Idaho. These bucks were okay by Wisconsin standards but not what Roy was coming all the way to Idaho for. The third week of November, 1997 his luck changed in a big way.

When Roy arrived, he was the only one in camp; my other hunters were not scheduled to show up for another two days. I asked Roy if he minded if I accompanied him into his Olevan hot spot even though he felt fine without a guide and I knew he really did not need me along.

Being a thoughtful and generous person he said, "Fine, why not carry your rifle and do some hunting too?"

I turned him down on the offer to hunt, but was happy to go along as "guide."

The ridge trail going into the head of the Olevan drainage was easy to follow and could be hiked in the dark with a flashlight. That is how Roy had usually gone in so he could be in his favorite place before daylight. On this particular day I suggested that we wait at the truck until it was light enough to shoot, then hunt our way in. I could tell that Roy felt a little reluctant to do this, wanting to get to his familiar area early and start hunting at daylight.

He agreed but asked in a doubting tone, "Well, where would you expect to see a buck on that trail?"

I had hunted the ridge trail and guided hunters there many times. I told Roy there were two spots where he should go slow and be on his toes. The first was about three-quarters of a mile from the truck. He would recognize it by a small spring above the trail and a stream that flowed across the trail and down the drainage to the east. For some reason only known to deer, I had often jumped deer near that spring. On at least two occasions, hunters and I had seen good bucks there. One had been bedded below the trail and spooked before the hunter could get a shot. The other was a buck that was walking uphill and the hunter shot and missed as the buck crossed the trail.

The second good spot on that ridge trail was about a mile farther in toward Olevan. I described to Roy where the trail cut to the left across a very steep hillside. Just beyond the steep part, there was a saddle where I had often seen bucks crossing. One of my hunters from western Oregon had killed a buck in that saddle a few years earlier.

With those particular spots in mind, Roy and I left the truck that morning just at daylight. Roy was to hunt the trail and I was to take a different route. We planned to meet in a pre-determined place around noon. There was no question that Roy was very capable of being on his own and my presence would only hinder him — more noise and more movement. Therefore, with our lunches in my daypack, and carrying my binoculars and camera, I took a route that would keep me away from Roy's ridge trail.

It was a rainy, dark day with no snow and little wind. I hiked an abandoned logging road that paralleled the ridge trail. This old road was not drivable and had started to re-vegetate with brush and small trees. In some places, the road and trail were a half-mile apart. In other places, they were as close as 200 yards. I felt sure that if Roy shot I would hear him.

Our plan was to meet at noon about two and a half miles from the truck. We would eat lunch, visit about the morning hunt, and then make plans for the afternoon.

I took my time and checked out familiar areas for buck sign. If I found exceptional amounts of fresh buck activity I would describe the areas to Roy and he could hunt these places in the afternoon.

About half way on my trek, I saw a small 6-point buck. He was feeding in a thick, brushy area just a few feet above my road. I was able to approach to within 20 feet before he made a startled jump then stood broadside and stared at me. I thought to myself, "If I were bow hunting this would be an easy one."

I dropped below the road into a 20-acre section of heavy timber between two logged areas to check for sign. As I entered this piece I jumped two large deer but I could only see glimpses as they bounded downhill through the thick trees. My sense was that they were a buck and a doe, though I hadn't gotten enough of a look to know for sure. This was mid-November and the rut was at its peak. Further into the piece I discovered lots of fresh tracks and droppings. The 20 acres was mostly steep hillside except for one small bench of flat ground in the middle. I stood in one spot on this 2-acre bench and counted five fresh scrapes and numerous rubbed trees. The place smelled of deer urine.

I immediately eased out and climbed back up-hill to the road. The discovery had me pumped up for Roy as much as if I were doing the hunting. I increased my pace, thinking I would get to our meeting spot well ahead of him. I didn't want Roy to waste any time so he could return to this "buck bedroom" below the old road. Unless he had discovered something better I was anxious to send him there.

My suggestion would be for him to drop off the road down to the 2-acre bench, then find a place to sit on the hillside above and wait for deer to move in. I would sit above him on the road to be there if he needed help and to accompany him back to the truck in the dark — always a welcome thing for any hunter.

I reached our meeting spot at about 10:30, well ahead of the planned noon meeting. To my surprise, I saw smoke curling up through the trees from a campfire. As I neared our rendezvous spot, there was Roy with his back against a tree and his feet up warming them by the fire.

Roy had left the truck and stillhunted the ridge trail as planned. He recognized the first good spot by the hillside spring as I had described it. He sat there for about 45 minutes overlooking the head of the small drainage. Seeing nothing, he moved on. The damp ground made stillhunting quiet and Roy felt good about the morning. His mind was on the headwaters of the Olevan drainage a couple of miles ahead but he forced himself to go slowly and stay focused. This was ground he had only traveled through before daylight or after dark and it now looked good to him.

At about 9:30 he was approaching the second "hot crossing" I had described. Again, he forced himself to slow down, walk quietly, and keep a sharp eye out for deer. On a straight place in the winding trail, he suddenly saw the movement of a deer. It was 75 yards ahead of him and below the trail. He only got a quick look—not enough to know buck from doe or even small from large. It looked to Roy as though the deer was moving uphill on a course that would take it across the trail 75 yards in front of him.

Roy's experience told him that an off-hand shot at that distance at a deer stepping across the narrow trail would be difficult. Trees and brush hid the deer and gave Roy only seconds to move. He bent over to make himself smaller and hurried forward to a big grand fir tree about 20 yards ahead and on the left side of the trail.

A persistent Green Bay, Wisconsin hunter on his 5th Idaho whitetail hunt with a nice 4X5 buck.

Roy wasted no time in resting his left arm and forearm of his rifle on the side of the large tree. He had time for two quick, deep breaths to steady himself. Then the deer stepped up onto the trail 50 yards ahead and stopped.

With no time to size up the antlers or to count points, Roy settled the cross-hairs on the buck's front shoulder and squeezed the trigger of his Remington Mountain rifle. It had been immediately obvious to Roy that this buck was the best he had seen in five years of Idaho hunting. The 130 grain Nosler .270 bullet hit the big buck in the front right shoulder and exited the left shoulder. The buck never knew that a hunter was anywhere near him.

Roy tagged, field dressed, and left the buck where he had killed it. He knew the two of us could drag it to the truck that afternoon. Then he hurried on to our meeting place.

As I approached Roy, I wondered why he was there so soon. I knew it was not like him to waste good hunting time warming himself by a fire, especially so near to Olevan, where he loved to hunt. On the other hand, I was glad to see him so I could describe the great afternoon hunt I had lined up for him. I had not heard any shots so it never occurred to me that Roy's hunt might be over.

As I got closer I could see blood on Roy's hands and his ear-to-ear grin told me immediately that he had killed a buck. Since it was his first day of a 6-day hunt, I knew it had to be a good one. He described the hunt as we ate an early lunch by the fire. I gave him a quick description of the hot two acres and my plans that were no longer needed.

Roy's comment was, "Well, this buck was headed in that direction but I interrupted his plans. We'll remember your hot spot for next November."

First-Day Buck

In 1998, Dr. Bob an orthopedic surgeon, came to hunt Idaho for the first time. He came with an old friend of mine and repeat client, Dr. Huck. Huck was a dentist who hunted with me over several years. Huck never came alone, always bringing a friend or relative to introduce to Idaho. He was the type of hunter who would rather have a hunting companion kill a good buck than kill one himself. He was about to experience this — in spades.

I liked Dr. Bob from the start. He had hunted, fished, and traveled all over the world. He was a good story teller and his adventures ranged from hunting stag in Russia to fishing king salmon on the Pacific coast. His yarns told me he was a down-to-earth guy who could fit in with any class of people in spite of his status as a surgeon.

Dr. Bob was a big man in his early 60's but could get around in the woods like a man half his size and age. I knew it would be a good week of guiding and I hoped the hunting would be good for him and Huck, too.

Our first morning out was one of those miserable days so common for Idaho in November. It was rainy and cold with so much cloud cover it felt as if we were hunting in an old black and white movie.

Before daylight, I walked Huck into a treestand I had placed in a big Douglas fir tree on a ridge. This stand was on high ground but a hunter could not see far due to the thick timber surrounding the stand. The great attraction of this spot was a primary scrape on a saddle only 30 yards to the right of the stand. There was also a well used game trail crossing the ridge directly in front of the stand.

The stand was heavy-duty, made of poles with a stout pole ladder. I had cut the material from dead trees in the area about four years earlier. The platform was only about two feet by four feet but had a pole railing on two sides and large trees on the other two sides. Even though Huck was nearing seventy years of age, this was a safe and comfortable stand for him. I never worried about putting Huck in these stands because he was a small, wiry man who was always in good physical condition.

Huck was not an enthusiastic treestand hunter. By his own admission, he had little patience for sitting; he preferred to stillhunt and was good at it. However, I knew that in this rain he would stay much drier in a stand than moving through wet brush. I left Huck in the dark and returned to the truck where Dr. Bob was waiting.

As was my usual routine, I planned for one hunter to be in a treestand for the morning hunt while I stillhunted with his partner. In the afternoon, the roles would reverse.

A word here about this practice of switching hunters: I learned early in guiding that having hunters alternate from stillhunting for a half-day to standhunting for the other half-day gave a pair of hunters more enjoyable hunts. They each experienced a greater variety of scenery and had less chance of getting bored. The stillhunter and guide were able to have short, whispering visits and get aquainted while having a serious hunt. The treestand hunter could generally tough it out longer, knowing that his turn for a stillhunt with the guide was coming. It was great for hunter moral but it could be hell on a guide, since this was a tiring method of guiding.

For me, it involved hiking a hunter into a stand in the predawn darkness using a flashlight, then hustling back to the truck. We would usually drive to a new area and stillhunt for four or five hours. It was up to me to keep track of time, get back to the truck, and drive to the stand location to hike in and retrieve the hunter. Sometimes hunters were able to come out on their own, but until they became familiar with the routes I had to go get them.

After lunch, I would repeat this process. The only difference was that for the evening hunt the treestand hunter would usually feel confident that he could find his way out in the dark. I would try to remind hunters to watch the route carefully on the way in because they would be on their own coming out. At that, some hunters would ask me to come and get them at dark. All in all, giving hunters this variety was great for them, but a tough way to guide.

With Huck settled in a good treestand, Dr. Bob and I concentrated on stillhunting though the rainy morning. We started a slow hike on an old logging road through some good buck country. This road was covered with tall grass and it was not long before we were both wet up to our hips. We found a place overlooking a hillside where we could watch for deer and stay relatively dry. My hopes were not high that we would see anything moving in the downpour but I didn't let Dr. Bob know how I felt.

I was wearing a wool coat and pants and was soon wet through to the skin. Dr. Bob had on some high-tech clothing that seemed to be keeping him drier, but far from comfortable. We moved a few times and rattled in a couple of places but generally just gritted our teeth and made it through a bad four hours. We returned to the truck looking and feeling like two drowned rats.

Huck was patiently waiting in his stand when I went to fetch him. He was no drier than we were, though the canopy of large trees had sheltered his stand. Huck had not moved from the tree and he was so cold I almost had to pry him from his seat and lower him to the ground. He was just getting the kinks out by the time we reached the truck.

The three of us huddled in the pickup with the engine running and heater on, trying to dry a little. Mostly, we just warmed up our wet clothes. The hot coffee and lunch made us feel better.

About 1:00 P.M. the rain let up giving us the boost we needed to head out on the afternoon hunt. As planned, it was Dr. Bob's turn to sit. We drove about two miles to a new location, higher up the mountain in the Meadow Creek drainage.

I sent Huck on a hunt by himself into an area he had hunted in past years. Huck was a quiet, patient hunter and perfectly capable of hunting alone. We had become close friends over the three years he had booked hunts with me and we enjoyed being out together as guide and hunter.

My plan was to join up with Huck after I got Dr. Bob situated. It took us about 20 minutes to reach the treestand. Again it was a permanent stand with the platform and ladder made of poles I had cut from trees in the area. It had a pole railing on three sides and a plywood roof suspended by poles. This was my most elaborate treestand and a great one for rainy weather. I had located it in a hillside strip of timber about 150 yards wide between two clearcuts. From this stand, a hunter could look uphill to the edge of a clearcut and downhill to the other clearcut. Any deer passing through this funnel of woods would give a hunter a reasonable chance for a shot.

I say "reasonable chance," since my hunters were not always able to get shots when bucks passed through. The funnel was thick with large trees and some brushy undergrowth; a hunter in the stand had to be alert in order to watch all 360 degrees. If he were daydreaming, a buck could be well past him before he noticed. This had happened more than once.

I left Dr. Bob about 2:00 P.M. and told him to stay as long as he could stand the cold, wind, and rain.

His words to me as I left were, "This looks like a great place and with this roof over me I will stay until dark. Don't worry, I'll get back to the truck on my own."

I hustled out of the area and headed to the trail that Huck was hunting. Huck knew I would be trying to catch up with him so he had hunted slowly. Within 30 minutes, I came up behind him as he was taking his time and doing more stopping and looking than walking. He was a hunter with lots of white-tail miles under his belt and he knew how to hunt. After whispering a quick "Hello," I let him know Dr. Bob was happy where he was and we could concentrate on hunting. We continued on the route, stopping every 100 yards or so and watching. We had both hunted this trail before and knew where to stop—we didn't need to talk about it.

As Huck and I eased over a gentle ridge and stopped to look things over, we both spotted a deer at the same time. Huck was ahead and I was peering over his shoulder. I tapped his back to let him know I saw the deer and he nodded to assure me he had also.

The deer was walking slowly up hill to our right and had not seen or heard us. Huck eased the safety off as his gun came up. I looked past Huck's head and could sight along-side the barrel as he followed the deer. These moments were as exciting to me as if I were the one with the rifle. The deer stepped into an opening at about 40 yards distance and I could see it was a buck but only a small 8-pointer.

I whispered, "Careful, too small" in Huck's ear and he nodded in agreement and slowly lowered the rifle.

We watched the buck walk out of sight up the hillside unaware of our presence. Then we continued our hunt.

Huck and I had only hunted for about 45 minutes when we heard a shot. Immediately, we thought of Dr. Bob. The shot came from his direction and, as the crow flies, he was less than a mile from us. The sound seemed to be the right distance and direction.

One of the great things about hunting whitetail in Idaho was the lack of other hunters. However, here was a case where there was a chance that another hunter was in the area and had shot. Huck and I talked about the possibility.

I said, " I think that was Dr. Bob but we can't be sure. We can keep hunting or we can go see, it's up to you, Huck."

He immediately said, "Bob wouldn't shoot at anything but a big buck, let's go help him."

After I had left the Doctor that afternoon, he quickly settled into his comfortable stand. He had a block of wood and a cushion to sit on and had his back to a tree with his rifle across his lap. He was only 12 feet off the ground but the steep hillside put him well above the deer trails on the downhill side. His back was to the uphill side and he could turn slowly to scan the ridge above him with the tree blocking his movements.

Dr. Bob was just getting into imagining the likely places where a buck might appear when one did. At first, it was just a movement about 30 yards to his left and at his elevation on the hillside. He knew it was something but it could have been a bird or a squirrel. Then a buck stepped out at a fast walk, on a route that would take him below the stand. Until that moment, Dr. Bob had not seen the game trail but now it was obvious.

Dr. Bob cautiously raised his rifle and followed the buck in his scope. He thought, "That is a good 10-pointer and it would be a great 10-pointer if it were back home." The Doctor hesitated. After all, this was the first day of a 6-day hunt in Idaho. He didn't need to prove anything by killing an average buck— he decided to let it go.

The buck had no more than gotten out of sight when Dr. Bob got twinges of "Did I make a mistake?" He started thinking "Why couldn't that buck have stopped and let me decide a little longer? I might never see a better one. What will Huck and Jack say?" After a few minutes he settled down and decided it was too late to stew over it. There would be another chance.

No more than 30 minutes later there was another chance; again, a glimpse of something, this time from the right. A large animal was moving from about the same place where the 10-pointer had dissappeared. Dr. Bob's first thought was, "He's coming back. I'll get that second chance to look him over. Oh man! I'll have to make a choice again."

Now he could see the buck and knew it was going to cross from right to left about 50 yards below his stand. There was no waffling this time. When the buck hit the first opening Dr. Bob knew instantly he was going to shoot. This was not the same buck!

With his huge neck and heavy blocky body he walked like a Herford bull and made the first buck look tiny. His antlers were high, with long points and beams jutting past the buck's nose. As the buck stepped into the third opening, the Doctor settled the cross-hairs on the monster's shoulder and touched the trigger.

A Maryland hunter with his beautifully mounted 163 B&C buck killed on his first day in Idaho.

The big buck shot forward at full speed. There was no chance for a follow-up shot. The Doctor was not new to hunting and his instincts told him there was no need. He heard a loud crack as the buck slammed into a tree on his death run. Dr. Bob could see enough of the buck to know it was down and it was over.

He tried to calm himself but his knees were not getting the message. He carefully gathered his pack, seat pad, and rifle and climbed down the heavy log ladder. On the ground, he had to force himself not to hurry, but to savor the moment. As he eased up on the buck he could see it was even better than he had thought. It was a beautiful 10-pointer with very symmetrical long white points and good mass. There was no doubt now that he had made the right choice in passing up the first 10-pointer. The Doctor let his knees shake and smiled to himself that after all these years and all the hunts he still got the "weak knees" like he had when he killed his first buck as a teenager.

It only took Huck and me 20 minutes to get back to Dr. Bob's stand. We were both relieved to see he was not in the stand. That told us he was probably the one who had shot. We quickly spotted him 60 yards below the stand working on his buck.

I was always a little apprehensive about checking on a hunter after hearing a shot. If he were not the one shooting then I would be disturbing his hunt by blundering back to check. This time I was very glad we went with our instincts.

The Doctor's buck scored 163 B&C and was one of the top five bucks our hunters killed. We were three very happy hunters. It is a tribute to Huck's graciousness as a hunter that he was as happy for his friend as if he had killed that big buck himself. For me, guiding these two experienced and grateful hunters more than made up for the wet, cold day and I forgot how miserable I had been. They were two more hunters who actually made guiding easy.

CHAPTER 5

Stick to the Basics

I had been guiding for about four years when a freelance out-door writer named Harry Morris called me to set up an interview. Harry heard my business was unique in the sense that I was the only licensed guide and outfitter in Idaho guiding exclusively for whitetail deer. He knew there were a few others in the state guiding whitetail hunters but most of them focused primarily on elk and mule deer. Elk has always been the big attraction in Idaho, followed by mule deer, mountain lion, and black bear. Most Idaho outfitters viewed guiding for whitetail as just an afterthought in case an elk hunter got lucky early and wanted to hunt something during the remainder of his hunt.

When Harry arrived I showed him some of my trophy whitetail heads and photos of bucks my hunters had taken. We talked about how I had gotten my start, how I ran the business, and about whitetail hunting in Idaho. He indicated that he was interested in writing an article about my guiding business, but gave no indication of what he had in mind for a story.

As we visited, Harry kept eluding to my techniques and methods for getting the good bucks that I had shown him. Apparently, my descriptions of how we hunted weren't giving him much to work with and he finally just came right out with, "Jack, I need to know your secret to success so I'll have an angle for a story."

Harry went on to explain that these days almost every whitetail article has some new twist for outsmarting big bucks. He

49

listed articles about patterning, mock scrapes, pre-season planning, after season scouting, and on and on. I was starting to get the picture but I had no catchy twist as a theme for his article.

I plainly said, "Harry, we don't have an angle, we just get out there, hunt hard, and stick to the basics."

With that I expected Harry to leave and find someone with an interesting angle to write about. Instead, I could see an idea forming in his mind and he said, "That's it, the story is that you hunt bucks the old fashion way, you work for them."

That was about as accurate a description of how we hunted as anyone could give. Harry went on to write two articles with that theme. One was published in *Deer and Deer Hunting* magazine and the other in *North American Hunting* magazine. I got a lot of hunter interest from those articles and they helped my business immensely. Best of all, I had countless hunters call me or write and say that they really liked the honesty and the no-nonsense approach that we took to hunting.

I guess it's human nature to try to find the quick and easy way of getting something. I am the first to admit that I like to dream of the novel ways I might be able to outsmart deer but alas, I have come to the conclusion that there are very few tricks, gimmicks, or gadgets that work consistently. If they did, we would soon have all the big bucks killed and become bored with the whole hunting sport.

It is tempting for an outfitter to give prospective hunters the impression that he has some edge on killing big bucks. Like any business owner trying to pay the bills, it is easy to get a little loose with the truth when trying to book hunters. I can tell a good story as well as anyone but I learned early that when hunters called to inquire about whitetail hunting in Idaho I had to be honest. The day-of-reckoning for an outfitter is about the forth day of a seven-day hunt, when hunters haven't seen anything bigger than a spike and a few does. That's the day when a guide wishes he would have been a little less free with the promises.

Fortunately for me the truth was a pretty good story. I would explain that my area was one of the best whitetail areas in the country. Compared to whitetail in most of North America, Idaho

This hunter had the tenacity to hunt hard for seven days, passed up several smaller bucks, and took this mature buck on her last day.

deer experience relatively low hunting pressure. This allows bucks to live long enough to reach their full potential of body size and antler growth. I don't think these deer are genetically programmed to be any bigger or better trophies, but they are able to live long enough to mature, which is essential for producing trophy bucks.

Deer harvest studies by the Idaho Department of Fish and Game confirm that 59 percent of whitetail bucks taken statewide are 8-point or larger and over 20 percent are 10-point or larger. When I detailed those statistics to hunters they quickly got the picture that Idaho has some good whitetail hunting. I went on to tell them that often my hunters, most of whom came from east of the Mississippi River, would shoot the first buck they saw in Idaho and it would usually be the biggest they had ever killed. This is understandable when you consider that, statistically, one out of five bucks is a 10-point or larger and more than one out of two are 8-points or larger. In addition, the deer population has a high percentage of bucks, hovering around a ratio of one buck for every two or three does. This all means that a hunter doesn't have to look at many deer to see a buck and he doesn't have to look at many bucks to see a shooter.

After pumping up inquiring hunters with these numbers, I would always bring them back to earth with the rest of the story. That was, not all of my hunters went home with bucks. In fact, over my 14 years of guiding, my client success rate was around 65 percent. In an area with little hunting pressure, a deer population made up of greater than 20 percent trophy bucks, and close to half the deer being bucks, why wasn't everyone able to get one?

Like guides everywhere, I have always viewed my hunter's success rate as a reflection of my guiding abilities. In my first years of guiding deer hunters I was frustrated that more of them were not going home with bucks. I remember thinking that it must be something I was doing wrong as a guide. If I could get better at placing treestands, learn my area better, or do more scouting, I could get this guiding thing honed finer and everyone would kill bucks. However, I finally came to the realization that regardless of how many mature bucks there were and regardless of how hard I tried as a guide, there were some elements of success beyond my control.

There were always hunters who's drive to get out and hunt was lukewarm. They had all the right equipment, and loved to be in on the planning, but when it came to getting out and hunting hard they lost interest. I often sensed that many of those indifferent hunters were not comfortable in the woods, had fears of getting lost or eaten by something, or may even have had some aversions to the whole idea of killing, gutting, and dragging. The difficulty for me as a guide boiled down to the fact that some of those hunters — for whatever their reasons — were not willing to put in the time.

Poose Dawes, an old and experienced whitetail hunting friend of mine from Pennsylvania, used to say about whitetail hunting, "You've got it about half licked if you just get into the woods and stay there." Those words always came back to me when I would put an unenthusiastic hunter in a treestand and within an hour he was back at the truck saying, "I didn't see anything, can we go to a good spot?" Or when hunters at mid-week of a six-day hunt would say, "Do we have to get up at 4:00 A.M. tomorrow? Seems awfully early?" These were often hunters who could talk it up over the phone but when it got right down to it they should have spent their hunting money on vacations to Las Vegas with their wives. They weren't willing to make the effort and they often went home disappointed.

The Basics

If half of hunter success has nothing to do with skills or abilities but only depends on a willingness to, as Poose said, "...get into the woods and stay there," what makes up the other 50 percent? It may sound overly simple, but based on my own hunting experiences, my observations of clients, and from what my guides have shared with me, a hunter's ability — or willingness — to be alert, quiet, and still most often means the difference between success and failure. I am convinced that these three fundamentals account for around 40 percent of whitetail hunter success.

Be Alert

The advantages of being alert while hunting should be as obvious as the advantages of being sober while driving. However, I've been amazed at how often I've seen hunters miss chances at good bucks because they weren't paying attention. On more than one occasion I have been able to read the story in the snow where deer had walked unnoticed past a hunter in a treestand. There have been several times when I have put a hunter in a tree before daylight and returned 3-4 hours later to find him not paying attention or even sleeping. I have spooked deer in plain sight of a hunter in a stand only to find out that he was not aware of the deer or of me returning to get him. A hunter who doesn't notice his guide, wearing an orange cap and vest and walking to his stand is not alert.

We often fall into the trap of thinking there are times to be alert and times when it doesn't matter. It was common for hunters, while walking with me into a stand or an area where we planned to hunt for the day, to walk as though they were walking through Central Park. They would watch their feet or look straight ahead down the trail and never see deer standing or bedded to the side. These were often hunters who were experienced and in most situations were alert and paying attention, but had a habit of turning their hunting mode on and off to fit the situation.

The reality is that when we are in deer woods there is always the chance to see a buck any time and any place. There are places and times that are better, but we miss opportunities if we start thinking that we know where it will happen and where it won't.

Be Quiet

The advantages of being quiet should be even more obvious than the advantages of being alert. An old Indian proverb comes to mind here: "A feather fell to earth. The eagle saw it, the bear smelled it, and the deer heard it." I think it would be safe to say that I never guided a hunter who would not have agreed with this adage. Most knew that being quiet was essential to getting a buck, but each of us has a different idea about what constitutes noise, how much noise we can get away with, and when we can get away with it.

I recall sneaking into an area with a young hunter, in his mid-twenties, from Wisconsin. He and his hunting partner were on their second trip out to hunt with me in Idaho. This young man had not gotten a buck on his first trip and had already missed a big buck earlier this particular day, so his spirits were low and I was trying very hard to get him a buck. I had explained that we were going into one of my favorite spots and that, from past experiences, I knew deer bedded in this area and there was always a lot of scrape activity about. Our plan was to be very quiet going in, then find a place where we could be concealed and where we could watch some well used trails and scrapes.

He had been treestand hunting, so I hadn't gotten any feel for his sneaking abilities. We moved through some thick, brushy areas and he was careful about where he stepped and how he eased through the noisy brush. All was going well.

After a few hundred yards without making any noisy mistakes, we got into fresh sign, two large scrapes, and a well used deer trail. The place smelled like bucks and we were both pumped with anticipation. I chose a spot for us to sit where we could see even though it was in heavy timber and a shot would be less than 50 yards. I quietly sat down with my back against a tree and motioned for him to do the same. After all this slow and cautious effort to get into this great looking spot without making a sound, he proceeded to break off limbs from the two trees in front of him to give him more room and a slightly better view. Some of these limbs were an inch or more in diameter and made enough noise to wake the dead. I sat in disbelief as he made his nest but I never said a word. It was too late.

We sat until dark without seeing a thing then hiked out to the truck. On the drive home he said, "I can't understand why we didn't see anything, it looked like such a great spot." This young hunter obviously knew how to be quiet but he seemed to miss the connection between quiet and seeing deer. He just didn't understand the basics.

My guide, Kelly Phillips, related a similar story of a hunter with his own ideas of what constituted too much noise. Kelly and this hunter, who was fairly experienced, sneaked into an area to watch the edge of a strip of timber where deer traveled between two logged patches. Kelly placed the hunter in a spot with a good view, then found a place about 150 yards away where he would be out of the way and out of sight but still near if the hunter needed him.

It was about 2:00 in the afternoon and the plan was to sit until dark. About every five minutes this hunter would clear his throat with a loud "haaack!" Kelly could easily hear this and after about 20 minutes could take it no longer. He got up and hiked over to this hunter to let him know that he was blowing his chances — Kelly was completely honest if not always tactful. As Kelly was about to whisper his advice, the hunter let out another "haaack!" Kelly said, "You know, when you do that, the deer can hear you."

With a puzzled look the hunter responded, "Oh, you think so?"

It's not always the mistakes we make but sometimes the equipment we choose that is too noisy. I always sent an "Equipment Needed" list to hunters before they came out for their hunt. It was a way of giving them some idea about footwear and clothing they might consider for a hunt in Idaho in November. On the list I stressed the need for quiet clothing made of wool, fleece, or some of the warm and quiet synthetic fabrics.

However, time after time hunters would show up with jackets made of nylon, or pants made of waterproof and breathable material, or a full set of plastic rainwear. These guys, who obviously ignored my list, would sound like a bride coming down the aisle in her layers of satin and lace. Often, before the hunt was over we would stop at the local logger's department store to buy wool coats and pants so they could finish their 6-day hunt in quiet clothing.

Often the guys who break the brush, talk too loud, or wear noisy clothing are just out of their environments, and what worked back home may not work hunting in a different area. Someone from South Carolina may have no idea that hunting quietly on frozen snow is almost impossible and that stand hunting is about the only recourse under those conditions. Wearing quiet clothing that can slip quietly through the brush may never occur to a hunter used to the open farm country of Iowa. And a western hunter who has no problem moving quietly over pine needles will appear to be a novice when hunting in the New England states on dry leaves. But the fact is, deer everywhere depend on their ears to avoid hunters and being quiet is a basic precaution that can't be overlooked.

Be Still

Being still is probably the easiest of the three basics to achieve but is often the reason for hunters going home skunked. It doesn't depend on equipment, the hunting conditions, or any special skill, all it takes is self-control. As with being quiet, being still often means different things to different hunters. I have sat in ground stands with hunters whose idea of being still was not standing up and sitting down more than four times in an hour. I have observed hunters who thought that squirming from cheek to cheek, scratching their ear, opening and eating a candy bar, and pulling up their sleeve to check the time were all part of being still.

Of course, it is almost humanly impossible to stay locked in an immobile position for more than an hour or two, and this is really not a good hunting technique, since a completely immobile hunter can only see what is directly in front of him. Turning your head from side to side can be done and should be done

Staying calm and making a difficult 200-yard shot got this Michigan hunter a good 9-pointer. The buck was in the middle of an Idaho clearcut.

but only very slowly. Also, scratching that unbearable itch or having that candy bar that you can't get off your mind can also be done but you must move like a sloth. I have seen deer, including big bucks, walk right up to my hunters when they were standing or sitting perfectly still. On the other hand, I have seen deer bolt and run when they spotted the quick turn of a hunter's head at two hundred yards.

The Moment of Truth

So far, we have accounted for 90 percent of hunter success; what makes up the final 10 percent? I call it being able to put it together at the moment of truth, that short time when a hunter sees a buck, knows it is the one he wants, and has to make the shot. It's the most critical time in the hunting process and the time when luck plays less of a role than at any other time.

Over the years I have seen hunters who were willing to put in the time and effort and who had a good grasp of the basics, but when the moment of truth arrived they were not able to make the kill. They were like golfers who can do all the right things to get the ball onto the green but blow it on the putt.

In almost every case the ability to do well when the pressure is on boils down to experience. Hunters who have grown up shooting starlings off the barn roof or killing rats at the local dump are those who do best in this critical time. Those real situations taught them subtle things about when to make their move, the need to be fast yet accurate, and how to shoot when excited.

A few years ago I was guiding a father and son from back east. The son was about 40 years old, not a kid by any means but very inexperienced. He had hunted very little and I doubt if he had killed more than one or two deer. In many ways he was a guide's dream; he was in good condition, never complained, followed directions to the letter, and was willing to do whatever I thought would get him a buck. To top it off, he was one of the nicest guys you could ever go hunting with.

One morning I put him into a treestand on a ridge that was always a good bet for traveling bucks during the rut. This was about the third week of November and the rut was in full swing.

We had gotten about six inches of snow the night before and it stopped snowing just before daylight, about the time I left him in the stand. The plan was for him to stay there until noon and then come out to the truck for lunch. His dad and I would hunt an area nearby and meet him at the truck.

This was a common schedule since it gave hunters a mid-day break, a chance to warm up, and a chance for me to see how everyone was feeling about the hunt. If we weren't having much luck we could move to a different area for the afternoon hunt.

His dad and I did some stillhunting and rattled in a few places but only saw a couple of does. We were back at the truck about a quarter to twelve. We had just started lunch when the son showed up. And was he excited! Since daylight he had seen five different bucks from his treestand. He went on to describe each buck in detail.

The first had come through shortly after daylight. It was a heavy antlered buck, kept its nose to the ground, and passed behind the treestand and disappeared to the hunter's right. The next three bucks had come from different directions and were of various sizes and descriptions. He said that at least one of these three was a very good buck.

The fifth buck had come into sight about 10 minutes before noon. The hunter's description of this one I remember clearly. He said, "It was a real big buck with lots of tall points sticking way up above its head." This buck moved through at about 75 yards (which is about as far as one could see in the heavy timber where this treestand was located) and appeared to bed down. The hunter related that he couldn't see the buck after it bedded but was sure it was still there. Not knowing what to do, he waited the few minutes until noon then eased out of the stand and sneaked out to the truck as planned.

As he told this story I became more and more puzzled about why he had not shot. I was sure that his father and I could have heard a shot from the treestand but we had heard nothing. This hunter was not holding out for a huge buck, in fact I knew from our previous conversations that he would be happy with most any buck. All of these deer had to have passed within less than

75 yards of his stand, some he had described to be within just a few yards, and all were moving slowly. I could hold off no longer and finally asked the obvious question, "Couldn't you get a shot at any of those bucks?"

His wide-eyed response was, "None of them would stop. The only one that did stop, bedded down before I had a chance to shoot."

This hunter was at a loss as to how he should have handled the biggest buck, the one that bedded. No one can say what would have been his best move but hoping to come back after lunch and pick up where he left off with this buck was not it.

Here was a hunter who was willing to sit for hours, knew enough of the basics so as not to spook these bucks, but because of a lack of experience and confidence, had not been able to make the right decisions at the critical time.

This story does have a happy ending, however. As we ate our lunches I gave him a quick lesson in shooting. I explained that it's great to be careful and to make a good clean kill but that a walking deer at close range is much easier to hit than he might think. I remember ending this Shooting 101 with the advice that if the cross-hairs are on the vitals and you feel good about it, just pull the trigger.

He went back to the stand and within two hours an 8-point buck walked through in front of the stand at about 25 yards. This hunter, with renewed confidence and some simple advice still on his mind, was able to put it together. He never saw the big buck that had bedded but was thrilled with the one he got.

Harry, the free-lance writer finally got it right in his magazine articles with the theme "there are no quick and easy angles for killing big bucks." In the final analysis, the best you can do is to get out of your truck and into the woods often, stay there as long as you can, and hunt hard. The time spent will increase your chances of meeting up with a buck and sticking to the basics will give you the advantage in that encounter. With increased experience and familiarity with your equipment you will be able to put it all together at the moment of truth.

CHAPTER 6

Two for the Record Books

A Boone and Crockett Buck

Guiding and hunting have one thing in common — the end results are very unpredictable. Hunting depends on the weather, the quarry, the equipment, other hunters, and just plain luck. Guiding depends on all those things plus the attitude and ability of the hunter. Guiding is among a very few activities where the one in control has such little control over the outcome.

When I would initially talk to a prospective hunter, I would try to size him up and form a mental picture of how the hunt might go. If I could guess correctly as to what kind of hunter he was, I could modify my guiding plans accordingly. Sometimes my picture was accurate but most often it was way off and my planning didn't help much. It's tough to admit, but hunts often just took their own direction and we followed. This unpredictability often meant sleepless nights for me, but it was what kept guiding interesting.

One evening in 1989, I was on the phone trying to size-up a guy from the Washington coast named Dave. He and his younger brother, Cecil, were interested in the upcoming fall whitetail hunt. They both wanted big bucks or no bucks at all.

I thought, "Okay, I've heard that a hundred times. I hope these guys know how tough it can be to get big bucks."

Dave went on to describe that he and Cecil were in their 60s, had never hunted whitetail before, yet wanted trophy bucks. This struck me as big talk for guys new to the sport. Never the less, I signed them up for a 6-day hunt during the third week in November. They were to buy their own Idaho hunting licenses and deer tags and drive over, rather than fly.

A few days before the brothers were to leave from the coast, they called with a problem. Cecil had lost his deer tag and was considering canceling the hunt. I explained that he could get a replacement at the Idaho Fish and Game office in Lewiston on Monday. After some debating on his part, he finally agreed to stick with the plan. Monday was the first day of our hunts and he would have to miss it — to get a new tag the law required that he purchase it in person. I could sense that he was not too eager to go through the hassle but at least I had changed his mind about backing out of the hunt.

The week that Dave and Cecil arrived, we had four other hunters in camp. Mark and Pat, two young hunters from Wisconsin, were in their 20s, had grown up hunting whitetails, and were not too particular about getting big bucks; they were here to have fun and see what Idaho hunting was about. Our other two clients, Jim and Jay, were from Washington and were middle aged with some whitetail experience. So, we had a wide range of ages and abilities but all easy-going guys and it looked like a good week ahead.

Kelly Phillips was guiding for me and this was his second season at it. I always viewed Kelly as a no-nonsense fellow who was very dependable. Kelly had more whitetail savvy than any hunter I had ever known, and I decided to put Dave and Cecil in his hands and I would guide Jim and Jay. My thinking was that the older brothers would appreciate Kelly's serious nature.

My other guide that year was Donny Ball, a local farmer and friend. Donny was new to guiding but he had grown up here and knew the areas we hunted well. Donny was to guide the young men from Wisconsin.

Dave and Cecil got to camp on Sunday. I had a short visit with Cecil that afternoon and I got the feeling that, at best, he was neutral about this hunt. He let me know that he had never needed a guide and had always been able to do fine on his own. It wasn't the first time I had heard older hunters, who were used to doing without a guide, express this attitude. Dave seemed to be the hunt promoter and his brother was just going along with the idea.

Cecil was the one guy in camp that week that I would have bet would not kill a buck. I'm glad I didn't put money on my hunch.

Early Monday morning, guides and hunters headed out. Dave and Kelly hunted, while Cecil drove to Lewiston for his tag.

The week progressed well but hunting was not great the first couple of days. On Wednesday, Donny and the Wisconsin boys broke the dry spell by getting a nice 5X5 buck with a drop-tine. Donny had organized a small deer drive and pushed the buck to Mark, who made a good shot. The next day Jay got a small 8-pointer.

Cecil, Dave, and Kelly were still plugging along looking for big bucks. Cecil had seen seven bucks but none of any exceptional size. Dave had seen three bucks and over 20 does. Saturday morning was the last day of their hunt and it was beginning to look as though the brothers might not get a chance at trophy bucks.

Kelly drove the two hunters into the Big Creek watershed. His plan was for Dave to hunt a logging road that would take him up a ridge on the west side of the drainage. There were many old roads and clearcuts to give Dave plenty of good hunting.

Kelly and Cecil were to head up another ridge that would take them into an area where Kelly had done some shed antler hunting the previous spring. The three would meet back at the truck around noon.

Kelly had been itching to get back into a basin near the headwaters of an unnamed tributary to Big Creek where he had seen old scrapes and rubs. He had never had a chance to hunt the area but it had struck him as being a good place to take a hunter. It required an uphill hike of about a mile and by the time he and Cecil reached the end of the road it was daylight. They still had a half-mile hike through timber to reach the basin.

Cecil was winded from the long hike and the men stopped occasionally to let him catch his breath. They were now in the timber and Kelly reminded Cecil that they could jump deer anywhere. On the third rest break they stopped in a nondescript spot—later when I asked Kelly if there was something special about the area he said with his usual composure, "No, just another place in the woods." They were standing about 25 feet apart, watching quietly for deer. They were hunting but their minds were on getting to the basin that Kelly had described.

Kelly thought he heard the faint sound of a buck grunt off to their left. It was so subtle he didn't alert Cecil. In a minute or two he heard it again and this time, he was sure. Kelly signaled to Cecil that a buck was coming. Cecil nodded in response.

Within a few seconds the buck appeared. It was walking slowly, grunting, and on a course that would take it within 40 yards of the hunters. The buck was traveling through heavy timber but there were plenty of openings for a shot.

Kelly immediately realized that this was a big buck. The antlers were tall and massive with multiple points. In any other situation, he might have focused on counting points and sizing up the head but his mind was on his hunter. He could see out of the corner of his eye that Cecil still had the rifle slung over his right shoulder, not ready for a shot. All Kelly could do was hold his breath and wait for Cecil to make a move, hoping the buck wouldn't see something or catch their wind and bolt.

Since the two men were not standing together, the buck had to travel a few yards before Cecil could see it. Finely, and with no apparent haste, Cecil slipped the gun off his shoulder, took a long deliberate aim, and fired. The 180 grain .30-'06 bullet hit the big buck high in the right shoulder and he crashed to the ground. The buck immediately started thrashing trying to regain his footing.

Kelly later described it saying, "The buck was flailing the ground with that huge rack and Cecil was trying to aim for a head or neck shot to finish it. I was afraid he would hit those horns and ruin them."

Cecil's rifle, an old custom-stocked gun on a Mauser action, had jammed after the first shot. After several attempts at working the bolt and reloading, it still would not fire. Luck was with

This 18-point buck scored 195 7/8 B&C points and was the 19th largest non-typical ever taken in Idaho.

them that day and the big deer finally expired without the need for a finishing shot.

This was the largest whitetail Kelly had ever seen up close. It was a basic 10-pointer with eight additional big non-typical points. Most impressive was the tremendous mass of the dark brown beams and points.

As they stood over the huge buck, Kelly was reminded that this was Cecil's first whitetail when the hunter turned to him and asked, "Kelly, is this a good one?"

The buck later scored 195-7/8 B&C points and is listed as the 19th largest non-typical buck from Idaho (*Records of North American Big Game, 11th Edition*).

This buck, like so many big ones our hunters killed, was totally unexpected. We had never seen him before, had not found his shed antlers, nor had we talked to anyone who had seen him. A hunt that had gotten off with a shaky start and that I had predicted might not go well for Cecil had ended with a buck for the record book. Once hunters started admiring this big buck it didn't take Cecil long to realize, "This was a good one."

A Pope and Young Buck

The following year I got a call from a Pennsylvania hunter named Roger. He had seen my ad in *Deer and Deer Hunting* magazine and wanted to book an archery hunt for 1990. I had never advertised for bow hunts and had actually discouraged the few archers who had called me. Archery hunting was not a popular sport in Idaho in those days. There were no early-season hunts in our region. The only archery hunt offered was a winter hunt that opened December 5th.

December in Northern Idaho can be cold, snowy, and brutal for hunting from treestands. I knew the difficulties of guiding in December so I tried my best to dissuade Roger from coming. I described the conditions he could expect and he insisted that he could handle them. I finally gave in and booked him for a 6-day hunt during the second week of December. Kelly and I crossed our fingers and hoped for the winter to start mildly.

The 1990 rifle season had turned out to be a good one for our guiding business. We booked 11 rifle hunters and they killed 11 bucks. These bucks ranged in size from modest 8-pointers to a big 6X6 that field dressed 202 pounds.

In those early days of the business, we booked 7-day back-to-back hunts, leaving no days between hunts for us to catch our breath. The season was long and hard but we sent home many happy hunters. *Idaho Whitetail Guides* had been in business only five years and we already had several repeat customers. Any doubts about whether we could give hunters their money's worth were gone.

Roger was to be the only hunter in camp that second week of December and Kelly would be guiding him. I planned to return to work at my job with the Idaho Department of Environmental Quality in Coeur d'Alene. Carolyn would stay at our deer camp and cook for the guys.

We had no portable treestands so Roger had four of his own shipped to Idaho. Kelly and I had ideas for good stand locations but we wanted to wait and include Roger in the final selection and stand placement.

Roger arrived December 3rd in order to have a couple of days to scout and work with us in putting up treestands. To our surprise, he unpacked a recurve bow and cedar arrows. We immediately realized that this guy was no ordinary bow hunter. When he took a few practice shots at camp, we were impressed with his shooting abilities. He was hitting 2-3 inch groups at 25 yards, consistently. Now, if we could just get him that close to a good buck.

Roger also dispelled our concerns about his being able to hunt in the cold and snow when he unpacked a full suit of heavy-weight wool camouflage clothes. We had never seen these before but we knew we were dealing with a capable cold-weather hunter.

During Saturday and Sunday we placed three of his portables in what we thought were our best locations. It was important that Roger be in on selecting the stand sites since Kelly and I had more of an eye for rifle hunting situations. We could pick good general locations for stands. Roger, however, knew what his limitations were and was able to select individual trees that would give him his best shots. We kept one stand in the truck as a reserve.

Monday, December 5th, was Roger's first morning to hunt and the weather was cold with clear skies. Kelly drove him to a long ridgetop in the upper end of the Gold Creek drainage. They walked together to within 100 yards of the stand. From there, Roger indicated he could find it in the dark.

The plan was for Roger to stay until mid-morning or until noon if he was warm enough and felt good about the spot. Kelly was never one to sit in the truck for long so he planned to scout some areas near by and check back at the truck from time to time. It was about a half-mile from the stand to the truck.

Kelly took his first scouting trip and returned to the truck in two hours. Resting across the back corner of the truck box, was a cedar arrow covered full-length in blood. The broadhead was missing but the arrow was not broken. Tracks in the snow told Kelly that Roger had been to the truck, left the arrow and headed back toward the treestand. Kelly grabbed his pack with camera and drag rope and struck out on Roger's tracks.

Before daylight that morning, Roger had found his stand using a flashlight. After climbing into place, he pulled up his Black Widow recurve and pack. As was his habit, he hung the removable quiver with cedar arrows on a hook at the left side of the tree. He hung his fanny pack on another hook on the right side of the big tamarack and settled in to wait for daylight.

It was a cold morning with the temperature around 10 degrees but the lack of wind made it comfortable. Roger felt good and planned to stay until noon. The ground was covered with three inches of old frozen snow. Roger knew he would have no trouble hearing deer approach in that crunchy snow. He could only see for 50-60 yards but he should hear them long before seeing them in the dense timber.

The stand was in a narrow strip of trees between two logged areas. As Kelly had explained when we hung the stand on Saturday, "This man-made funnel should be a good travel route for bucks. The rut is tapering off but, hopefully, some are still traveling looking for does that didn't get bred."

The main game trail through the strip was 20 yards in front of the stand. Roger noticed that there were no apparent fresh tracks made on that trail since we put the stand up two days earlier. That was discouraging but it was the first day of a 6-day hunt and nothing could dampen his optimism.

Daylight slowly brought the Idaho woods to life. A red squirrel chattered in a tree to Roger's left. Several small birds flitted from tree to tree checking bark for tiny meals invisible to Roger. These birds were not like those he was used to seeing from his treestands in Pennsylvania. He was becoming mesmerized watching them until he was snapped into focus by the sounds of deer approaching from behind.

A less experienced hunter might have turned quickly to look, but Roger forced himself to turn like a sloth until he was looking over his left shoulder. There stood a large doe with head up checking the air with her nose. Roger could only feel a faint breeze but it was blowing in her direction. His immediate hope was that his scent would be blowing over her since he was 16 feet above the ground. She, apparently, was getting some whiff from his tracks, which were now an hour old.

Behind the cautious doe appeared two smaller does then a fork-horned buck. All four deer went into a semi-alarmed mode and, for a moment, Roger thought they would blow up and run. He was not interested in shooting but their presence would be great for attracting other deer, maybe bigger bucks.

The little buck finally changed the picture but not by bolting. Instead, he put his head down and ran at one of the smaller does like a teenage boy not sure of the difference between love and play. This scattered the does and the old one seemed to relax. All four deer then fed slowly below Roger's stand until they were 50 yards to his left.

He was again settling into the scene, watching the forky as he continued to pester the does. Then in an instant, the little buck's demeanor changed from bully to a scared interloper. He threw up his head and stared directly toward Roger's tree. To his right, Roger could hear the crunching footsteps of another deer. Roger remained stock-still. If he moved to look, the little buck would surely see him. He didn't have to stand still for long. The newly arrived deer was on the game trail and walking fast in a beeline toward the group of deer.

As the deer came into view, Roger immediately thought, "This is the buck I came all the way to Idaho for." There was no time to admire the big buck as he was quickly passing directly in front of the stand at 20 yards. As the buck's head went behind a tree, Roger drew his bow instinctively and waited until the deer stepped into the open. The Zwickey-tipped cedar shaft caught him behind the shoulder and disappeared through the deer. The big 8-pointer gave a quick kick with his left hind leg as though stung by a bee. Then he bolted forward into the other deer and scattered them.

The woods returned to silence. Roger sat down in his stand for the first time that morning and tried composing himself to

A Pope and Young record book buck taken with a recurve bow and cedar arrows by this traditional archer.

assess the situation. It had happened so fast. As he sat there, he spotted his arrow and his heart jumped. The cedar arrow with its two gray-brown feathers and white cock feather was stuck in a big fir tree on the far side of the trail. Could he have missed? Then he saw blood in the game trail and realized the 65-pound bow had driven the arrow through the buck with enough force to stick into a tree on the opposite side.

Roger sat for a few minutes enjoying the morning and reliving the moment. Then he climbed down, pulled the cedar shaft from its tree-imbedded broadhead and started tracking. The steady stream of blood made the trail easy to following. The buck made it just out of sight of the treestand before he went down.

Roger had hunted Idaho for less than two hours but he had memories to last for years. The buck scored 142 Pope and Young (P&Y) points and was the largest Roger had killed in his 12 years of bow hunting. He summed it up when he said, "You don't know if it will happen in the first hour or the last hour. It's the 'not knowing' that makes it so much fun."

CHAPTER 7

Hunting Methods for Guiding

Driving Deer

Any time someone mentions deer drives my thoughts go to northern Wisconsin in the 1950s and '60s. As a boy learning to hunt deer, driving seemed as natural as hunting snowshoe hare with a beagle or smoking raccoons out of hollow trees—it was the only deer hunting method I was aware of; how else would you do it? Driving deer *was* deer hunting.

Of course, that was half a century ago and many things were different then. One big difference was that most of the farm and timberland was open to hunting. We seldom asked permission to hunt and rarely saw a "No Hunting" sign. Landowners were local folks and, with few exceptions, we knew them and knew it was okay to hunt their lands. The country in Washburn and Sawyer Counties was a patchwork of hardwood forests and cultivated fields. Most of the timber stands were from 40 to 80 acres in size and laid out in neat squares or rectangles, making them easy to drive.

Back in the 1950s, there were fewer hunters in the northwoods of Wisconsin and most folks hunted in groups and only hunted by driving deer. Those groups were referred to as "gangs" (if any remain today, I doubt if they use that name). Our group, the Skille Gang, was made up of 8-10 relatives and included my father, sister, brother and me plus an uncle and 2-3 cousins.

The only other large, local gang was referred to as the Preacher's Gang. It was made up of the local Methodist minister and several members of his congregation who were hunters. These two gangs hunted the same general area and often made the same drives. There seemed to be a loose agreement and respect between our gangs and we rarely interfered with one another.

Driving worked well because we were all familiar with the land and we knew where the deer bedded and where they were likely to come out when pushed. As a youngster, I helped with the drives before I was old enough to carry a rifle. Then, at the age of 12, the legal hunting age at that time, I was ready to take my place as one of the hunters. Most of the members grew into the gang as I did and that early learning made for a smooth functioning group of hunters.

Gang hunting provided a great learning experience for a beginning hunter. First, it provided the ultimate in Hunter Safety Education. There were no classes on the subject as there are now but we all learned our gun handling lessons. The older members of the gang watched the younger hunters like drill sergeants watching new recruits. The slightest infraction of gun safety brought a swift and not-too-gentle reprimand. During my years guiding in Idaho, I was able to draw from those early lessons when I had to remind hunters of the absolute need to be safe. Gun safety was a non-negotiable subject back in the gang as well as during my guiding days, 30 years later.

The gang and the drives gave me my first lessons in deer behavior, shooting, tracking, and taking care of the animal after the kill. It gave me my basis for ethical hunting which has not changed much since then. Above all, it kindled an early love for deer hunting that burns as bright today as it did all those years ago.

So, it was not surprising that I included deer drives as one of my methods of guiding. In my initial years with clients, it was a fairly successful method and many of the big bucks killed in those first years were bucks I had driven to hunters.

However, it did have one big drawback. I didn't have my old gang to help, and had to do all the driving myself. On top of that, I had to walk the hunters to their stands and then return to the other end of the piece to make the drive. After the drive I would gather the hunters, then go on to another drive. It didn't take long for this one-man-show to take its toll on me. I found myself wearing out before the 7-day hunts were over.

I quickly learned to use deer drives sparingly and only in special situations. I often combined driving with stillhunting or treestand hunting. Since I usually guided two hunters at a time, I could station one hunter in a ground or treestand location where he had a good chance of seeing deer. The other hunter and I would then stillhunt toward the first hunter or hunt slowly in a large circle around him. This was not a typical drive but it increased the stand-hunter's chances of seeing deer.

This kind of hunting often took 2-3 hours after which we would repeat the method in a different area with hunters switching positions. It was less tiring and made an interesting day of hunting for the clients. It was much easier for a hunter to stay on a stand knowing that someone was out there stirring up deer. Conversely, it added to the excitement of stillhunting knowing that if we kicked-up a deer the treestand hunter might get a shot even if the stillhunter did not.

Though it was physically demanding for me as a guide, driving deer to hunters was always rewarding. It gave me a feeling that I was actually able to make something happen for my hunters. One of my most memorable drives occurred in 1986, my second year in the business. I had not hired other guides at that time and was doing all the guiding myself.

My wife, Carolyn, and I had done a lot of scouting during August and September that year. We specifically looked for areas with good deer habitat that also provided some chances of pushing deer to hunters. Those areas were not common in our Idaho guiding area; much of the whitetail country here consisted of large expanses of timber with steep terrain. Pushing deer and expecting them to go to a hunter was like flushing quail and guessing where they might land.

We located several deer drive possibilities throughout our 460 square mile assigned area. I was not planning to make drives continuously, but I wanted the options to be near if needed. In many cases, Carolyn and I actually made the drives that fall to get some feel for where deer might go when pushed. She would take a stand in a likely spot and I would push through to her. We used surveyor's ribbon to flag the ambush locations so I could find them later.

Our first hunters that fall came for a 10-day early November hunt. These were George and Linda, a husband and wife hunting pair from western Washington. They had hunted whitetails in eastern Washington, so were somewhat experienced, but had never been on a guided hunt.

The weather was warm for November and we hunted the first four days on dry, noisy ground without any luck. We were seeing small bucks and does but these folks were after big bucks and I was learning fast how tough guiding for whitetails could be. I was hoping to build a good reputation in those first years so I could draw more hunters and make a success of the business — this hunt was not helping my record.

I had no treestands, it was too dry for good stillhunting, and this couple did not have much patience for standing in one place. I resorted to making drives in those areas that Carolyn and I had checked out earlier. I was 40 years old then, had been doing lots of running that summer, and could cover Idaho's hills and thick timber without much effort. These folks made the drive method easy since they were good at following directions and good at picking the most likely places where deer might come through.

After two days of making drives from dawn until dusk without anyone getting a shot at a good buck I was becoming discouraged, though I tried not to show it. I had learned years earlier in helping my father guide hunters in Wisconsin that above all else a guide must keep an optimistic attitude. If his clients sense that he has lost hope, their morale falls apart quickly. Moreover, a hunter who thinks he is not going to score, usually doesn't.

We got about an inch of snow the sixth night of the hunt. It was not enough to quiet the woods for stillhunting but enough so we could see tracks and make the drives more interesting. At first daylight that seventh morning, I sent this couple in to take stands on an old logging road. I described the lay-of-the-land and where I would be coming through on this drive. It was up to them to pick the most likely places to intercept deer.

This particular drive was not through heavy timber but through an area that had been logged a few years previously. There were no trees larger than six inches in diameter and not many of them. The only good cover were scattered clumps of 6-8-foot-tall grand fir trees.

As I started through this drive, I zigzagged to cover as much of the area as possible. I soon struck the tracks of a big deer traveling alone. The tracks had been made earlier that morning after the snow had stopped falling. As I followed this deer I came to a scrape, then another — he was obviously not far ahead. These scrapes were fresh and his tracks were going in the direction of my hunters. My hope was that he had not already passed through.

As I continued to follow these huge tracks into one of the fir thickets, I heard the unmistakable heavy ground-pounding sounds of a big deer as he blasted out the other side. This buck had bedded in the firs and would have watched me walk by if his tracks had not taken me to him. I checked the bed and it was big like the tracks.

He was headed in the right direction and my hunters were not far ahead but he was going at full speed. Now success depended on whether they had picked the right ambush spots and whether they could hit a big buck making 20-foot bounds.

In less than a minute I heard one shot, then silence. I followed the tracks until I saw George standing on the old road. The tracks showed that the buck, still making long leaps, had crossed the road about 60 yards from my hunter. My heart began to sink as I feared that a 60-yard shot at a running buck would more than likely result in a miss.

As I approached George, I could see a slight grin and a twinkle in his eye — not signs of a hunter about to tell a sad story. His first words were, "I hope you won't be disappointed."

Here was a rare hunter. He was as concerned about his guide

The author (left) put on a one-man deer drive to this veteran hunter who made a tough 60-yard shot at a fast bounding buck.

as he was in getting a good buck. He knew I had worked my tail off that week and he could sense that my frustration was building. He did not want to disappoint me by shooting a buck that was not a trophy.

We got Linda from her ambush position and regrouped before taking up the track. George went on to describe that the buck looked big but was going so fast that he was not able to judge the antlers as well as he would have liked to. The deer looked so immense that George had made a quick decision and shot. He also had no idea where he had hit the buck, if at all.

We tracked the buck into the timber and immediately found blood. In another 50 yards, we found the buck where he had made his last 20-foot jump. The shot from George's .300 Winchester Magnum had hit squarely in the lungs — a great shot at a running buck. The buck was a beautiful 4X5 with heavy beams. The big rack looked small on this huge bodied deer. He turned

Guide Kelly Phillips organized a 6-man drive that netted this lucky hunter a huge whitetail buck.

out to be one of the heaviest bucks in my guiding career. He field dressed 221 pounds. This was the first time, as an Idaho guide, that I had been able to actually form a plan and see it result in getting a good buck.

In the years following that unforgettable drive, I learned new hunting methods that made guiding easier, but I never completely abandoned driving. When conditions made stillhunting difficult and when hunters were too impatient or the weather too cold for stand hunting, I would head for one of my good old areas and make a drive. I always let my hunters know this was not something to expect every day and that it was to be viewed as a treat. I felt they should know that any time a guide makes a drive, he is going beyond what is expected.

The practice of driving deer has always had its critics. It is considered by some to be non-sporting or even unethical. I even read the occasional article where someone seriously proposes disqualifying driven deer from being entered into the B&C or P&Y record books. I have guided a few hunters who did not want to participate in the method, feeling it was not part of the fair-chase principle.

Those are valid opinions but, as hunters, we need to be careful not to be too judgmental about other hunters and their methods. As a hunting fraternity our methods are open to criticism by non-hunters who don't know and love the sport. The last thing we want is to find fault with each other.

Stillhunting

More of our hunters killed bucks while stillhunting than by any other method including deer drives, rattling, treestand and ground stand hunting, and the use of calls. We did not keep records of comparable hours spent hunting these different ways but I am quite sure that our hunters clocked more hours of stillhunting than any other method. That may be the obvious reason why it paid off. I personally don't think it is the best of the methods, but I'll get to that later.

The term "stillhunting" is an old one and is a little misleading, especially to late generations of deer hunters. It means to move slowly through the woods, stopping periodically, with the intentions of catching the deer feeding, bedded, or moving unaware of the hunter. It does not mean to stand still, which of course would be stand hunting.

Some hunters stillhunt at a pretty fast pace and if they are very alert and good at running shots they can be successful. I have a friend who stillhunts about as fast as I walk down a sidewalk. He has learned to travel quietly, he knows the country very well and knows where to expect deer, he covers a lot of ground, and he is a terrific shot at running deer. He has killed several nice bucks this way. He also has absolutely no patience for sitting still. He has helped me pick out treestand locations for my guiding. When he would say, "I like this place, I could probably stay here for at least 10 minutes," then I knew it was a good spot.

These young, energetic hunters could stillhunt at a fast pace over many miles of whitetail country in a day.

Most hunters, including the majority of those I've guided, stillhunt at a pace that will take them over a mile of ground in somewhere between one half to two hours. The pace depends on the terrain, the density of cover, the amount of deer sign, as well as the ability of the hunter to spot deer. The very best stillhunting conditions are after a fresh snow of two to six inches. In these conditions a stillhunter can move at a faster pace, cover a lot of ground, see deer much better against the white background, and do it relatively undetected.

I often hear hunters talk about stillhunting at a pace of only two to three hundred yards per hour. I know a couple of local deer hunters who cover only a mile of ground in an entire day. Their thinking is that they will be able to move so quietly that they will catch deer completely unaware.

I am leery of this approach. I don't believe that covering so little ground gives enough chance of an encounter with deer. It may make some sense where deer densities are very high but in the majority of deer country, including here in Idaho where deer numbers are less than 15 per square mile, a hunter must cover much more ground to bump into deer. To my way of thinking, these extremely slow moving stillhunters are no more effective than if they were to take a stand and continually squirm.

The secret to good stillhunting is to strike the right balance between moving fast enough to cover plenty of ground but slow enough so as not to make excessive noise and to thoroughly look over new areas encountered.

While guiding, I would sometimes send hunters off on their own to stillhunt. This worked fine if they were good at keeping their bearings. On more than one occasion, however, hunters became hopelessly turned around and I had to track them down in order to fetch them back to the truck.

If hunters wanted to stillhunt but were not comfortable alone, I would go with them. This had the disadvantage of two people making noise and movement. However, it had the benefit of two pair of eyes to spot deer. We would move slowly with the hunter in front, ready to shoot. I recall numerous times when I spotted bucks while looking over the shoulder of a hunter. I would whisper "there's a buck" and point past the hunter so he could sight down my extended arm and finger to locate the deer. Shots were usually close and if the bucks were unaware of our presence, kills were fairly easy.

Calling Deer

Today there are several deer calls on the market. They range from buck grunt tubes to fawn bleat calls. The grunt calls sound very close to the real thing. Some of the doe and fawn calls do not resemble anything I have heard coming from wild deer.

Like rattling, I did not use calls in my early years of guiding in Idaho. Over time, I grudgingly tried several calls and started seeing some results. I had bucks respond to grunt calls — but not as enthusiastically or as often as the sales hype would like us to believe. I remained convinced that calls should be used cautiously and at the appropriate time and place. I developed this conservative approach to the use of calls through my own trials as well as observing my hunters using them.

Nearly every year I had a hunter or two show up with the latest mail-order catalog's version of a deer call. The only knowledge these hunters had about their calls was what they had read on the instruction sheets that came with the calls. Those instructions were a good start in how to use a call but I didn't think a guided hunt in a new area was the right time to be learning.

I recall one November a few years ago when I was guiding a hunter from Michigan who had shown up with a fawn bleat call. This particular call was new on the market but had been advertised heavily and, if you believed the sales pitch, this thing would "bring 'em in from miles around." The call was a simple reed-call similar to a cow elk call—to my ears it sounded the same. I could not quite make the connection between sounding like a fawn in distress and attracting big bucks but this hunter explained that curiosity was the motivating force at work with this call.

The week that this fellow was hunting was one with very good conditions. We had fresh snow almost every day to help visibility and quiet the ground. The rut was in full swing and we could not have asked for a better hunting situation. This hunter did not care for treestands so most of our hunting was slow stillhunting with long periods of standing where we could watch good deer areas. Bucks were on the move and I was sure that it was just a matter of time before we would cross paths with one.

Our only problem was the deer call. Without fail, just when we would get into a good spot and things had settled down, out would come the call and the bleating would begin. This thing was loud and every raven, magpie, and jay for a half mile around would show up to see what was killing a fawn.

I am a patient man and for the first couple of days, I said nothing. I was curious about how deer might react to this new call and I honestly thought it might pull in does. If does came, bucks might be close behind. However, it didn't seem to be working. We were doing everything right and under these conditions of snow and the rut we should have been seeing deer. At first, I suggested that we use the call a little more sparingly.

I urged this hunter to try calling just before we got up to move to a new location. Eventually, I suggested that we not use it at all. But, he was convinced that calling would pay off.

On the last day of his hunt, we crept into an area in the Poorman Creek drainage where I had seen good buck sign. We were on a brushy ridge with a network of trails and plenty of rubs and scrapes. It was difficult to see more than 50 yards since the thick brush and trees were heavy with snow. We picked a spot where we could stand, leaning our backs against an up-rooted tree. Staying on our feet would give us a chance to see from all directions and the hunter could shoot better than if we sat. There was no wind and the snow-cover made the place deathly quiet.

We had discussed the use of the call and my hunter, who I think was finally starting to have doubts himself, had agreed to not use it. We were just going to let things happen. We had been there about an hour when we both spotted a doe feeding slowly toward us. Then behind her appeared two more does. They fed quietly past us at about 30 yards and were totally unaware of us. This was the best buck attractant we could have asked for.

I was excited and I was hoping my hunter knew the fortunate situation we were now in. But, his mind went to the call. I could not believe my eyes when he pulled it out of his pocket, slowly slipped it to his lips and started bleating. The does had come to us from the right on a trail, passed directly in front of us, and had moved to our left. When they heard the call all three of them, immediately, locked in on us. They started stomping and blowing.

My eyes were on the does but I caught some movement to our right down that trail. Another deer had been about to come into full view when the racket started. At first, I couldn't see the deer's head but at 40 yards, I could see it had a big body and large, dark tarsal glands. This big deer stood listening. I put my hand on the hunter's shoulder to indicate for him to stop bleating but, of course, it was too late. The deer had been alerted and he turned and retreated on his backtracks. As he did, I got one quick look at an enormous set of antlers.

The does moved off, still blowing and stomping and we waited with dwindling hopes that the big buck would settle down and return. I even rattled before we left, on the off chance I could bring him back, but it was over. My hunter had no idea just how close he came to having a shot at a very big buck.

That was his last day and he flew home the next morning. I had one free day before my next hunters arrived so I went back to that brushy ridge and put up a portable treestand in the exact spot where we had seen the does and the big deer following them. Two days later one of the new hunters was in this stand before daylight. At about 9:00 A.M., a doe came bounding through with a huge buck behind her. This hunter got the buck and it was one of the largest 10-pointers killed in our years of guiding. There was no way of knowing if this was the same buck that we had chased off with the deer call but I always felt it was.

Doe and fawn bleat type calls may be helpful in bringing curious deer closer or luring them out of cover for a possible shot. However, I do not recommend blowing away on these calls (the same goes for handheld calls that don't require blowing) just anytime or anyplace in hopes of bringing in a buck. They all too often may have the effect of alerting deer to a strange intrusion into their familiar world.

My conclusion after years of seeing my hunters trying grunt tubes and experimenting with them myself is that they should be used discreetly. They should not be used when everything is going your way but, rather, when nothing else seems to be working. For instance, when a buck is obviously leaving the area and there seems to be no chance for a shot, grunting may turn him back.

I often blew a grunt call together with rattling since the two seemed more realistic to my hunters but I don't think it made much difference to bucks. I rattled them in both with and without the accompanying grunting.

My Favorite Guiding Method

I mentioned earlier in this chapter that more of our hunters killed bucks by stillhunting than by any other method. That exceptional success was in part, due to the fact that they clocked the most hours stillhunting. They were eager to try it since it was an exciting way to hunt; the scenery was constantly changing and there was little chance for monotony to take over. Generally, stillhunting satisfied their innate desire to see what was over the far ridge or around the next bend in the trail.

However, on a deer-per-hour of hunting effort, I am convinced that stand hunting was the most productive. Treestands had obvious advantages over ground stands but either were better than any other method we used in our guiding business.

Treestand hunting was also the easiest guiding technique that we used in our business. The stands required pre-hunt scouting and considerable work ahead of time to build, but once they

Treestand hunting paid off for this hunter from New York State. The buck was a heavy antlered 4X5 and was shot at less than 30 yards.

were up, guiding was relatively easy. When we could get hunters to spend time in them, they killed bucks.

Stand hunting eliminated two of the basic problems associated with stillhunting: noise and movement. Treestand hunting also reduced the problem of scent, to some extent, since the hunter's scent was carried away above deer's level and not detected. Stand hunting also gave hunters the advantages of being able to see and hear deer in advance. They could then be ready to make the shot. That was a definite advantage for inexperienced hunters who tended to get rattled at the sight of a big buck.

Ask any whitetail guide and he will tell you that stand hunting can be very effective. However, he will also tell you that one of the biggest problems in guiding is getting hunters to stay in their stands. Not may hunters can tolerate being cold, stiff, and "rump sprung" (as a friend of mine calls it) for hours on end. Even fewer can endure the boredom. We all suffer from that undeniable human trait of quickly talking ourselves into doing something else when we get bored. For my hunters, that something else usually meant returning to the truck for their coffee and sandwiches.

The bottom line in our guiding business was that if hunters could overcome the physical and mental challenge, there was no better method of killing bucks than hunting from a tree or ground stand.

CHAPTER 8

Old Guide, New Tricks

I feel a little embarrassed about the subject of rattling for whitetails. It reminds me of saying I wouldn't be caught dead having my bird dog in the house—like the one that now sleeps on my bed. When I was in my teens and getting my deer hunting start in northern Wisconsin, I learned to always be quiet in the woods. I never talked above a whisper, never slammed the car door, and never even coughed for fear of getting that "can't you be quiet?" look from my dad or older brother. So, I certainly was not about to crash antlers together, rake them on trees, and pound the ground with them. I spent the next 30 years pooh-poohing the idea and telling my hunting friends, "Rattling might work in Texas but I'd never try it up here; it just won't work."

Until the 1970s, very few hunters had heard of the concept of rattling antlers to attract bucks. Even the so-called experts didn't rattle for deer, nor did they speak highly of the idea. George Mattis was the local guru on whitetail hunting in northern Wisconsin when I was growing up there. In 1969, he wrote a very popular book called *Whitetail — Fundamentals and Fine Points for the Hunter*. George was a friend of my father, and George and his brothers hunted some of the same ground that we did. The book is 35 years old now and is still a good basic "how-to" on whitetail hunting.

In the book, George gives us a good picture of the thinking about rattling common to that era, especially in the Mid-west. He devotes only one small paragraph to the subject and sums up rattling with, "The attracting of deer by antler rattling for a close shot is productive in the Southwest, but it is largely experimental elsewhere." That described my thinking until one day in November 1990.

I had booked R.L. and Dennis, two young hunters from Alabama, and they arrived the third week in November for a 7-day hunt. This was their first trip out west and their first guided hunt of any kind. Their hunt immediately got off to a shaky start when R.L.'s luggage, including his rifle, got stranded somewhere between Alabama and Idaho. I loaned him my extra hunting clothes — right down to the long underwear — and my rifle. Some hunters would have opted to stay in camp until their luggage arrived but R.L. was not about to miss a day of hunting.

The first day out was one of the rainiest days I had ever experienced in November. It was a cold rain and to make it worse the wind was blowing strong from the northwest. By 2:00 P.M., all three of us were wet to the skin and very cold. We returned to camp and changed into dry clothes, had some hot coffee, and warmed up. We were all ready to call it a day but I had an idea for a quick hunt. We didn't have much daylight left and it was still raining so I suggested that we just take a drive. My policy was to never "road hunt" but that day, with such nasty weather, I made an exception.

By the way, anyone not familiar with Idaho's hunting laws would be surprised at how liberal they are, especially those dealing with guns in automobiles. As I write this in 2003, hunters can still legally carry loaded and uncased guns in a vehicle. Most of the guns you see hanging in the back windows of pickup trucks are loaded, some with live rounds in the chambers. Hunters cannot shoot from a vehicle or from the road, but if they get out and step off the roadway, they can legally shoot. These liberal laws make road hunting easy and it is a very common way for many folks to hunt deer and elk.

As a guide with liability concerns, I never allowed my hunters to have their guns loaded in the vehicles and I did not make it a practice to hunt while driving. Besides being dangerous, a major problem with hunting from a rig is that it's hard to know whose property you are passing through. However, it was common to see deer while driving between hunting spots. I generally would not stop if we saw a buck—it was the easy way to avoid getting into ticklish situations.

We had not driven far from camp that afternoon when we saw a large buck coming down a brushy ridge. He was about to cross the muddy logging road as we drove around a corner. When the buck saw our rig, he whirled around and headed back up the ridge and out of sight.

We were on federal land well away from major roads so I stopped and let the hunters out. I had hunted that ridge before so I had an idea of how to head him off. I sent R.L. up the left side and Dennis up the right. I told Dennis to watch an open saddle about 200 yards up the ridge. Of the two hunters, I knew that only Dennis would have a view of the saddle. I parked the truck and waited. In less than three minutes I heard someone shout, "He's going your way," followed in a few seconds by a shot.

A dandy buck that was spotted from the road. Where and when we encountered a good buck was never predictable.

When we spooked the buck he had dropped off the left side of the ridge into thick cover and had stopped. R.L. jumped the buck and forced him back to the ridge and across the open saddle. By that time Dennis was within 75 yards of the saddle and made a great shot at a running buck.

This was not the kind of "hunting" any of us were planning; however, the buck was a very respectable 10-pointer with long points and good mass. This spur-of-the-moment hunt required little in the way of guiding or hunting skills but Dennis made a difficult shot and we were all happy for him.

As the week progressed, the rain let up and R.L. and I continued to hunt. We were seeing bucks but R.L. had his heart set on killing a big Idaho buck and he passed up several small ones. One day in particular, Thursday I believe, we stillhunted all day and saw seven bucks. A couple of these were 10-pointers but did not have enough point length or mass to suit R.L.

We were beginning to wear out from stillhunting so on Friday I suggested that R.L. try a treestand for a change. I put him in the stand before daylight and we agreed he would stay until 10:00 A.M., when I would come and get him.

On that Friday, Dennis was with us so he and I sat in the truck visiting and talking hunting. We got on the subject of rattling and Dennis said he had some luck with it back in Alabama. Being the skeptic that I was at that time, I blew him off with, "It just doesn't work here in Idaho."

His response was hard to argue with, "What is there to lose? Let's try rattling when we go back to get R.L."

For lack of anything better I reluctantly agreed, but added, "I hope R.L. won't mind all the racket."

We had to drive back to camp to get some antlers since I certainly didn't have a need to carry any. I had a pile of shed antlers, which we sorted through until we came up with a big set of matching 5-points. If I were going to waste time with this business, I wanted to at least impress folks with my rattling horns. I tied them together with a short piece of rope and we headed back to get R.L.

At 10:00 A.M., we quietly approached R.L.'s treestand from

down wind. When he spotted us, I held up the antlers to indicate we were going to rattle. R.L. gave us a "thumbs up" as acknowledgement.

I had asked Dennis to do the rattling since it was his suggestion and he had done a little back home. He started clashing that big set of horns very aggressively and to me they sounded like they would chase every living thing from the area. I remember thinking, "This is the most ridiculous thing I have ever been a part of."

Dennis had rattled for less than a minute when I saw R.L. raise his rifle. I was just starting to wonder, "Is he pulling our legs?" when his rifle fired and I saw the flash of a deer turning to run. The brush was too thick for Dennis and I to see the buck approaching, but R.L. was in a perfect place to see and to take a shot.

As it turned out, R.L. hit the buck through the lungs. He was shooting a Ruger Model 77 in .270 caliber with 130-grain bullets. The dandy 5X6 buck ran about 75 yards and piled up. Later,

A treestand hunter from Alabama (right) and his hunting partner with a buck that came to "rattling". It was the author's first experience with this method.

R.L. told us that the buck came in at a fast walk heading straight toward the rattling. As R.L. raised the rifle his nylon vest made a swishing noise, causing the buck to stop in an opening. That gave R.L. a good, standing broadside shot at about 30 yards. If the buck would have stopped in thick cover when he heard R.L.'s vest, it is anyone's guess as to what could have happened.

R.L.'s gamble in waiting for a big one paid off. He was happy to have passed up bucks all week to get this buck with 11 points plus a couple of sticker points to boot. I was slowly becoming a believer in rattling but as my mother used to say about me, "He is too darned ornery to admit it." I could have passed this one off to beginner's luck but my belief in rattling was about to become cemented.

On the way home to hang up and show off the buck, R.L. mentioned seeing another buck that morning. At about 7:30 a buck had passed through to the east of the stand. He said that it was moving in heavy cover and did not give him enough time for a shot. R.L. thought it was a good size buck and he was certain it was not the same buck he shot at 10:00.

We had another hunter in camp that week named Bob who was from Rhode Island. One of my guides, Donny Ball, had been with him all week and they were not having much luck. The next day was Saturday, Bob's last day. That evening, with encouragement from Dennis and R.L., I asked Bob and Donny if they would like to try a re-enactment of R.L.'s success. They were game to try.

Donny and I walked Bob to the treestand before daylight and left him. I gave Bob the same directions I had given R.L. the previous morning. I told him to stay until 10:00 A.M. and I would be back to get him. However, I added, "Before you get down, Donny and I will rattle."

I was trying to hide my misgivings about this whole situation. Here we were back to a spot where less than 24 hours earlier we had fired a shot, tromped around, gutted a deer (the gut pile was about 75 yards from the tree), and dragged the deer out. All this time we were talking and taking pictures and taking no precautions about leaving scent. After this, would there be any chance to rattle up another buck? I was doubtful, but R.L. and Dennis had Bob so sure it would work that there was no turning back.

As planned, at 10:00 Donny and I returned and hunkered down in the same spot where Dennis and I had rattled. Donny had never rattled before so it was up to me. Bob could see us and appeared to be ready. I rattled that set of horns like I knew what I was doing, even though it was my first attempt. After about 30 seconds I paused and waited a minute, then resumed rattling. I had just gotten started on the second chorus when Donny and I saw Bob raise his rifle and fire. After the shot he threw his red hat into the air and let out a loud "all right!"

The buck had come in from a different direction than R.L.'s the day before and had stopped at about 60 yards. Bob made a clean shot and the buck only ran 40 yards. The buck was a perfect 8-pointer of modest size but had an 18-inch spread and was one of the prettiest bucks taken by our hunters that fall.

After 30 years of doubt, I had just witnessed two bucks enticed to rattling in two successive days, and both were killed from the same stand. I was now convinced and from that time on I used rattling as a big part of my guiding. Now, after another ten years and many successful kills attributed to rattling, I have a much better appreciation for when and how it works. Rattling, like any other method of hunting whitetails, obviously does not produce results every time. There are dozens of fruitless attempts for every successful rattle. Nevertheless, contrary to what my dad's old friend George Mattis wrote, it does work beyond the Southwest and is more than just experimental.

I went on to rattle over a dozen bucks with those same big 10-point sheds. Every buck brought in was a thrill but a few were particularly unforgettable. By the way, I found it not uncommon to have does and fawns come to rattling. Unlike bucks which tend to come in fast, does come cautiously as though they are more curious than excited. In addition, my experience indicates that small bucks are more reluctant to come to rattling; those few that did, came cautiously like the does.

The most spectacular rattling hunt occurred when I was guiding Greg and Jesse, two brothers from Vermont. In previous scouting that fall I had run into a series of heavily used scrapes in a creek bottom that ran through an old logged area. There was a high ridge on the east side of this creek and a low, flat basin on the west side. The area had been logged about 10 years earlier so it was grown up with head-high trees and had lots of old logging slash, treetops, and blow-downs. This made for a difficult area to quietly stillhunt, but was perfect for rattling.

I sent Jesse to hunt a ridge to the north with plans to meet at the truck around noon. Greg and I eased into this creek bottom from the south until we started seeing scrapes. There was no snow but the ground was wet from the previous night's rain. The scrapes appeared to have been worked since the rain and big tracks were fresh. I motioned to Greg that we should find a place to rattle and I whispered in his ear, "Looks like we are in this old boy's backyard."

Greg nodded with a smile as he hid himself behind a clump of fir trees. The hiding spot overlooked a little one-acre open area at the bottom of the slope dropping off that west ridge. The opening was probably a log landing used by the previous logging operation. I quietly eased in behind him and got ready to rattle.

I've concluded that "set-up" is more critical in rattling than how you actually use the antlers. I believe that if a buck is in the right mood anyone can entice him by any technique that vaguely sounds like a buck fight. If he is not in the right mood, no amount of rattling skill will do it.

When a buck comes, the hunter must be set-up right so as not to be seen, yet be able to shoot. If you are working in pairs, the hunter should be concealed but in a position, preferably standing, where he can turn easily to shoot. I have rattled in situations where the hunter sat on the ground. When the buck showed up the hunter was not able to shoot without making excessive movement.

It is often tempting for hunters to kneel, thinking they can see better than sitting and still be hidden. However, few of us can stay comfortable very long in a kneeling position. We can not help but to move after a few minutes of misery. Keep in mind that a buck coming to rattling is going to be aware of the slightest movement.

The person doing the rattling should hunker down so an approaching buck cannot see his movements. I like to sit in heavy cover just a few feet behind the hunter. This way I'm hidden but can see the movements of the hunter and even communicate in whispers or subtle hand signals.

I had hit the horns together for only a few clicks when we heard running on the east ridge above us. The snapping and popping of brush was so loud I thought we had spooked a couple of elk and they were getting out of the area. I stopped rattling to better hear and immediately realized the animal was running down hill toward us. Whatever it was, it was not trying to be quiet or sneaky. It came down through the logging debris like an Angus bull coming to grain.

I think Greg and I both realized it was a buck before we saw it dash out into the middle of the open basin. The big 12-pointer

Some bucks came cautiously to "rattling."
This fine 6X6 buck came on a dead run.

stood looking and listening trying to determine who was fighting in his "backyard." Greg had his rifle, a Ruger Model 77 Ultralite, to his shoulder but didn't shoot. The buck was too close and too alert for either of us to make any move or sound. All I could do was sit and wonder why Greg wasn't shooting.

In the next instant the buck was off on a fast lope and was starting up an old skid trail to our left. Greg fired when the buck was out of my view and I had no idea if he had hit him or even come close to hitting him. It looked like a difficult shot from my position. All I could think was that Greg must have frozen and passed up a standing shot. I had only met Greg the day before and had no idea if he could hit a running buck.

I asked Greg two questions before we moved, "Why didn't you shoot when the buck was standing?" and "Do you think you hit him?" His replies were encouraging. Greg explained that the buck stopped exactly where a tree in front of Greg blocked out the buck's entire chest area. At less than 40 yards Greg thought about trying for a neck shot but gambled that the buck would step forward. He almost lost the wager when the buck took off at a run. His second answer made me feel even better when he gave me an emphatic "yes!"

The buck was easy to track since he had run up the old grass covered trail. I could not see blood but his tracks were clear in the soft muddy ground. We found him dead only 30 yards up the skid trail. The .270 bullet had caught the big buck in the middle of the lungs.

Greg had done all the right things. He had waited for the buck to stop when it first appeared. I have guided many hunters who would not have had that control upon seeing such a set of antlers. He waited for a better shot when the buck stopped instead of trying for an iffy neck shot. After all this excitement, he made a terrific shot at a running buck — never an easy thing to do.

That buck gave one of the most aggressive responses to rattling I have ever witnessed. He not only came immediately but also charged in at full speed.

Rattling is easiest when working in pairs like Greg and I had done, but it can be done alone with good results, though handling both a rifle and antlers can get tricky.

One November I had a free day between outgoing and incoming hunters and I decided to try rattling a buck for myself. I knew of several hot spots with good potential but they were scattered throughout my guiding area. Because of the driving and hiking time between these places, I would only be able to hit four or five of them in a day. Therefore, I chose to spend all day in one area rattling and moving.

I headed for a drainage on the north side of the upper Palouse River where I wouldn't have interference from other hunters. From daylight until mid-afternoon I kept up a steady routine of rattling and moving. I would rattle for about 30 seconds, wait 30 seconds, rattle for 30 seconds, and then wait for about five minutes and move on. When I moved I would hike (not stillhunt) from 200 to 300 yards, then set up and go through the rattling sequence. I tried to move far enough each time to be beyond the range of hearing from my previous location. The distance varied with the terrain and density of vegetation.

When rattling alone, one of the difficulties that quickly becomes apparent is handling a rifle and antlers; it takes two hands to rattle and two hands to shoot. The method that worked best for me was to sit with my rifle across my lap. When I stopped rattling I would quickly lay one antler on the ground on my right side with the tines up. I would set the other antler on top of the first with the tines down. Then I would take my rifle in both hands and wait. If I heard a deer or saw one where I couldn't get a shot I could cautiously pick up the top antler with my right hand (still holding the rifle with my left) and rattle it against the antler on the ground. I learned early in the game that if I leaned my rifle against a tree or laid it on the ground I could easily get busted when a buck sneaked in and caught me only holding antlers.

By around 2:30 that afternoon I had rattled at about 30 locations without being able to catch the interest of a buck. My route finally took me to a small timbered bench on a hillside. Here the trees were one to two feet in diameter and their crowns shaded out most of the understory. Without disturbing the bench, I could see a couple of scrapes and several rubbed trees. I got situated behind an old whitepine stump to give me cover and began to rattle. I went through two of my 30-second rattles then laid the antlers down and held the rifle ready. I could see about 50 yards in front of me but to my left trees blocked my view beyond 20 yards—close quarters for a buck encounter. I was afraid that if a buck appeared I would not be able to make any movements.

After a couple of minutes I eased my right hand down and softly rattled the antlers on the ground. Suddenly, without a sound, a buck appeared from my left. He was walking with his head down as if tracking then raised his head and looked directly at me. He was now 15 yards from me but my old Model 70 was at my shoulder and my elbows were on my knees. If he saw any movement, it was when I slid the cross-hairs to his chest and pulled the trigger.

Hit hard with the 180 grain .30-'06 bullet he made a blind run in a half circle and went down. He was a beautiful 10-pointer

A light colored 10-point buck the author "rattled" to himself. Handling rattling antlers (shown in foreground) and shooting take some practice.

with 9-inch G-2s and 8-inch G-3s. He was a long, rangy buck built like a greyhound and he had the lightest straw color of any buck I had ever seen.

I have killed bigger deer but I will treasure this buck and the memories of the hunt more than any other because I rattled him. As hunters we are usually the ones chasing after bucks so it is a special feeling when we can turn the tables and get one of them to come to us.

I have come a long way from the skeptic I used to be on the subject of rattling. It only took a couple of successful kills to make me a believer. In the remainder of my guiding years, rattling became part of my bag of tricks right along with treestands, stillhunting, and the occasional deer drive. I've learned to "never say never" and that you *can* teach an old guide new tricks.

CHAPTER 9

Rodent of Bear Dog Ridge

B y 1994, I had 10 years of guiding under my belt. I had guided hunters who had been on hunts all over the world, hunters who were on their first trip, hunters with much more experience than I had, and hunters who had never killed a whitetail. As a guide, I was beginning to view myself as a salty dog that had heard and seen it all. That tenth fall I had booked Brian and Chris, two hunters from Massachusetts, for their first hunt in Idaho. They were to arrive in November for a 6-day hunt during the rut. I was about to learn that there is no end to what a guide might hear and see.

I had spoken with these guys a few times over the phone and felt I was getting to know them. Chris was in his 60s and Brian was about 20 years younger. They both seemed like nice guys with reasonable expectations and a willingness to follow my directions and advice.

Though their temperaments and personalities were similar, their hunting abilities and experience were worlds apart. Chris had hunted everything from Dall sheep in Alaska to boar and stag in Russia. He let me know that he was very comfortable hunting alone and would need a minimum of direction. Without bragging, he gave me the feeling he was a good rifle shot, would know how to quickly judge a trophy and could stay cool when an opportunity presented itself. Chris's standards were high. With his vast experience and numerous heads in his trophy room, he expressed his perspective by saying, "I really have nothing to prove. I love hunting and unless I see the buck of a lifetime, I don't need to kill one."

In contrast, Brian was a greenhorn. I didn't press him on the issue but I believe he had hunted very little and may never have killed a deer; he never offered up any stories. However, he was young and in good physical shape and what he lacked in experience, he seemed to make up for in enthusiasm. Brian had a modest goal: to kill a buck, just about any buck.

Though he did not expressed it outright, I had a sense that Brian was not going to be comfortable alone in the woods of Idaho. He had lots of questions about getting lost and the chances of meeting a bear or mountain lion.

This was a common affliction among hunters I guided. The whitetail country in Idaho is "big woods" to eastern hunters who are accustomed to hunting the "back-forty." Much of Idaho's deer country, with its vast tracts of forest, deep wooded canyons, and dark, dense timber can give a newcomer feelings of entering a Steven King novel. Fears can range from getting hopelessly lost to being eaten by some critter and never being seen again.

When guiding two hunters, it is difficult and unproductive to hunt as a threesome. Each hunter can be with the guide some of the time but each should be able to go-it-alone. Knowing what I did about these hunters, I put a lot of thought and extra effort into preparing for this hunt. From my standpoint, it was not going to be easy for Brian to get a buck. Sensing that he would be apprehensive when it was his turn to go on his own, I made some plans I thought might help in the upcoming November hunt.

He indicated that he would do fine hunting from a treestand. He told me that he would also be agreeable to stillhunting if I could assure him that he would not get lost.

With that in mind, my wife Carolyn and I set out to make easy-to-follow trails that would give Brian a way to stillhunt with very little chance of getting lost. One of the areas we selected for hunting trails was a high unnamed ridge above Little Sand Creek, a tributary to the Palouse River. I had killed a buck on that ridge in 1991, three years earlier, but had not been back since.

One day in late July, four months before Brian and Chris were to come for the hunt, Carolyn and I headed up the Palouse where we were able to drive to within a couple miles of the ridge. Then we carried our trail brushing gear the rest of the way on a logging road that was not drivable. Our objective was to spend the day scouting for treestand locations and opening up hunting trails.

One of the trails we chose to open was an old road that contoured the north slope of the ridge and ran through the heavy, dark timber where my 1991 buck had come from. The road was made sometime in the early 1900s, providing access to a hillside mineshaft. Idaho has several of these old mines, which were dug into the mountains by gold prospectors.

The horizontal mineshaft was still open, though the timbers were rotten and the mine looked unsafe to enter. An old wooden wheelbarrow and piles of rotting timbers were left near the entrance, much like the day the mine was abandoned. The old road that passed the mine ended about a fourth of a mile beyond and was barely visible, with brush and trees growing in the roadbed. However, it was a level surface in this steep country and made an ideal stillhunting trail once we brushed out a path.

Carolyn agreed that it would be a good hunting trail but thought it a little eerie with the old mine shaft, the dark timber and the remoteness of this "road to nowhere" as she described it. I recall her saying, "If you send a hunter alone down this trail he'll think he is being sent to the dark side of the earth."

Using a gas-powered brushsaw, I cut a 4-foot wide swath while she tossed aside the brush and debris. As I cut and Carolyn cleared a path, we soon had a great hunting trail. In places the trees and brush were so thick the trail was essentially a tunnel through the woods. At about 50-yard intervals I cut openings in the sides of the trail so a stillhunter could peer either up or down slope to watch for deer. Also, several game trails crossed the old road. At these trail intersections, we cut shooting lanes.

When completed, the trail made a loop about two miles long. A hunter could leave the logging road (the one providing walk-in access to the ridge) and hunt the old mining road for about one mile as it contoured the north slope of the ridge. After passing the mine shaft the trail eventually left the mining road and cut down a finger ridge for another half mile then turned left and came back to the logging road. The jump-off and return points on the logging road were about a mile apart.

Carolyn and I also chose two good treestand locations that day. One obvious site was where I had killed the buck in 1991. At another saddle about three fourths of a mile down the ridge, we selected the second treestand site. We cleared shooting lanes, pruned tree limbs, and marked the locations with colored ribbons for the fall hunt.

While working on that second treestand location, we had an unexpected visitor. A large black and charcoal colored Plott hound came trotting down the ridge to us. The dog training bear season was open and it was obvious that this old boy had been running for a couple of days. We could count his ribs and his belly was shrunk up like a greyhound's. Carolyn gave him what was left of our lunch and he wolfed it down without tasting.

We had been discussing a name for this unnamed ridge and now it was certain—we christened it "Bear Dog Ridge." When we left the area, we took the old hound with us in hopes of finding his owners. About 4 miles down the main Palouse River road we stopped at a camp of bear hunters. Sure enough, the brindle hound belonged to them and they were glad to have him back.

In mid-November, Chris and Brian arrived. I had been looking forward to this hunt and I was anxious to test the trails and treestands on the remote ridge. I hoped they would appreciate our efforts. The first day of their hunt was cold and overcast, with no trace of snow on the ground. The woods would be crunchy and visibility in the heavy timber would be poor. We headed for Bear Dog Ridge, with its new treestands and newly brushed trails.

As we drove up the Palouse River in the pre-dawn darkness, I explained how I had dicovered this area a few years earlier. A remote ridge above the Palouse River, it was hunted by elk hunters in October but was too out of the way for most deer

Jack Skille with a good mature buck he killed while late season scouting for new guiding areas.

hunters. I told Chris and Brian that one day, back in 1991, I had hunted the ridge to see if it had potential as a guiding area. I had immediately found that one downside to the ridge was the difficulty in reaching it. The best hunting appeared to center around a section of the ridge about two miles long and about three miles from the main Palouse River road.

I went on to tell them the following story in hopes of stirring their interest in hunting the ridge. By mid-afternoon on that day in 1991, I had seen several large scrapes on the ridge and some good treestand locations. One saddle near the upper end of the ridge had an incredible number of fresh scrapes. I had done enough exploring for the day and decided to take a stand overlooking these scrapes. It was snowing large, wet flakes and there were 2-inches of sloppy snow on the ground.

I continued to relate my story, describing that about a half-hour before dark a buck appeared from the heavily timbered north side of the ridge and walked into the middle of the group of scrapes. I was only able to get a view of his left antler, then a rear view as he started walking away. The points looked long and I could see good mass but I had no idea how many points he had or what the right side looked like.

I took the only shot I was going to get. The 180-grain .30-'06 bullet caught him just to the left and about four inches below his tail. The big buck started to crumple at the hit but managed to regain his feet and disappear down the ridge. I followed his blood trail in the wet snow and caught up to him in about 60 yards. He was still on his feet but about out of steam. A second shot to the lungs put him down. He turned out to be a 5-6 year old buck and field dressed 170 pounds. His antlers had four points on the left and five on the right with good mass and a 19-inch spread. His longest points were nine inches. I was thrilled to find that he was a better buck than my first quick look had indicated.

I finished my hunting story about the time that we reached the end of the drivable road. It was still dark but Brian and Chris were anxious to get started. I think my big buck story was helping to get them in the hunting spirit.

Not to get sidetracked here but I've got to tell you something about how guiding changed my perspective as a hunter. Once I started guiding, I never hunted quite the same again. I found myself constantly looking at the woods through the eyes of a guide. I would ask myself questions like, "How would I get a hunter into this place? Where could one hunter take a stand while the other stillhunted? How would I get a buck out of here? Are there any trails to follow or ridges to hunt or logging roads that would help a hunter stay on course?" These could have been distractions that interfered with my hunting, but I have always loved the planning part of hunting, so for me it only made hunting more interesting.

From where we parked that morning, we had to hike over an hour in the dark to reach the ridge. We stopped several times to cool down and I used these breaks to describe the plan. I gave a general description of the ridge and trails, and told Brian and Chris that I had been into the area a couple of weeks earlier putting up the new stands. I told them that I had seen lots of buck activity both near the stands and along the stillhunt route. I told Chris I would put him in the upper ridge treestand where I had killed the buck three years earlier. Brian would hunt the newly opened trail.

We reached the mining road trail as the morning was beginning to dawn. As I described how the trail wound through heavy cover, the openings along the way, the game trails, and the old mineshaft with artifacts near the entrance, I sensed a feeling of apprehension from Brian. I could tell by his questions that he was worried. In a serious voice he said, "Will I be able to find my way? Is the trail easy to follow? How long is this trail? How will I know when I am at the end?" He also made comments about the thick cover, the darkness of the timber, the overcast day and how far we were from the truck.

I reassured him that he would be fine and that he should take his time. I said that the trail could be hiked in 45 minutes but to do a good job he should stop and look as much as possible and take at least four hours to complete the hunt. I pointed out that there was very little wind so his scent would not be much of a problem but it would be very quiet and any noise would give him away.

Brian said good-bye and started on his hunt. I hiked Chris to his treestand and wished him luck. I had time to kill, so I dropped off the south side of the ridge and hiked the slope. I always enjoyed these times alone to look for deer sign, maybe find a shed antler, and just have time away from the pressures of guiding. However, my hunters were always in the back of my mind. I would keep track of the time and try to imagine just where they were on their route or how they were doing in a treestand.

This day I checked my watch often and hoped Brian would be okay. I even wondered if it would have been wiser to put him in a treestand on his first day out. I wasn't worried about Chris. He was an old pro and I knew that if he got cold he would climb out of his stand and hunt his way down the valley to the truck.

As I waited for Brian at the lower end of his loop, I felt sure he would see deer. I hoped to hear a shot—the sound a guide lives for. This remote area got virtually no hunting pressure from local hunters. I did not feel the deer density was high but there was plenty of buck sign. In an area like this with little hunting pressure, I had hopes that Brian would bump into a big mature buck.

My hopes sank when I finally saw him enter the clearcut above the road and start picking his way down the steep slope. I was relieved to see he had been able to find his way but disappointed he had not gotten a shot.

As he approached I could see a slight smile but he was shaking his head as though somewhat disappointed. "Well, I'm happy to see you were able to follow the trail," I said. "What did you think of it?"

As he caught his breath his first words puzzled me. In a slightly shaky voice he said, "Jack, you are not going to believe what I just experienced."

We sat down and he began to relate every detail. He told me how he forced himself to go slowly and do lots of looking. He even repeated my advice, "I did more standing and watching than walking." He described how he worked his way through the "tunnel" Carolyn and I had brushed out and how he stopped at every opening to watch for deer. He admitted that he had been excited at the possibilities and at the same time more than a little fearful of being alone on this dark, foreboding trail in the middle of nowhere.

About a half mile along the trail where the tunnel closed in and visibility was only a few feet, Brian said he heard an animal moving on the hillside above him. The sounds of snapping twigs and the crunch of footsteps were followed by what Brian described as "a strange, weird grunting sound."

He had never heard anything like it. The only thing that came to his mind was some kind of rodent—in his words "a very large rodent." Since he could not see anything, Brian continued to sneak along the trail. To his surprise, the animal was traveling about the same speed as he was and on a parallel course on the hillside above him. When Brian stopped, the creature would stop. At about 2-3 minute intervals, it would make the grunting sound.

With a feeling of curiosity mixed with fear and anxiety, Brian continued on his course. He told me he was sure the animal knew he was there and he soon got the impression that, for whatever reason, it was not running away but actually following him. What little wind there was blew down slope toward Brian, preventing the animal from scenting him. The two paralleled each other for about 150 yards until Brian's tunnel opened up on the uphill side of the trail and he felt like he was crawling out of a culvert.

He knew the animal had to be near and as his eyes began to search the timbered hillside above his trail, Brian's throat was dry and his heart was pounding. Then he saw what appeared to be a large rodent sitting upright on a 3-foot diameter moss-covered log about 30 yards up the slope.

I had hunted and scouted this area enough to know exactly the spot Brian was describing. He was looking uphill into a grove of mature cedar and fir trees about an acre or two in size. Some of the trees are 3-4 feet in diameter and their crowns block out most of the sunlight. In addition, this is a north slope, so the ground is damp with moss and ferns but little brush or small trees. This park-like pocket, for some reason, had more deer sign in general and more buck sign in particular than any other part of the north slope of Bear Dog Ridge. It was a spot I had described to Brian where he might stop and watch from the trail.

Brian told me, "As my eyes focused on the creature, I could make out the gray body and white chest. I could see its mouth and as I strained to make out more detail its lips moved and out came that same strange low grunt sound."

It then became clear to him that he was looking at large ears and antlers spreading out beyond those ears. Brian said, "It wasn't until that moment that I gave any thought to the possibility it might be a deer. I wasn't looking at a rodent perched on a log but the neck and head of a large buck looking back at me from behind the log."

His surprised reaction was to back up into his trail tunnel to gather his wits. He told me he then peaked out of the side of the brushy tunnel through a small opening and could see the buck walking straight away. He watched it walk up the slope through the cedar grove and out of sight.

At that point in his story I could not help but ask, "Weren't you able to get a shot?"

Brian replied, "I think I was so relieved that it wasn't a large rodent that the thought of shooting never entered my mind."

After pulling himself together Brian continued on his hunt past the old mine entrance turning left down the well-marked trail. He acknowledged that he had difficulty concentrating on hunting through the remainder of the loop. His mind was on the large rodent that miraculously turned into a trophy buck. He did not appear to be disappointed in the least about not shooting — just happy to be out of the woods.

Since that bizarre hunt I have thought much about just what took place in Brian's mind on that Bear Dog Ridge trail. I've come to realize that Brian was as much out of his element as I would be in a back alley in New York City. He was not comfortable being alone in this remote area. It was a dark and somewhat foreboding day. My descriptions of the trail and the old mineshaft may have added to his discomfort — perhaps turning it to fear.

Brian had never heard a buck grunt before, and in fact was not aware that they made any vocal sound at all. For some strange reason, his mind conjured up a vision of a large rodent and that was all he could think. From the buck's standpoint, Brian may have been a doe to court or another buck to fight.

Brian and I both gained something from that day. I know he felt a little foolish in having been so quick to make a wrong interpretation about what he heard and saw. He told me later that he now knew the sound of a grunting buck better than most hunters did and would never be fooled by one again. He promised himself that the next time he would stay cool and think about using his rifle.

The rest of the week went better for Brian, as he proved to be a much better treestand hunter than a stillhunter. He could sit from daylight until dark with only a short break to come to the truck for lunch.

By Wednesday, the weather turned cold and windy and it

started snowing. This made for tough treestand sitting but he never complained or gave up. On Friday he killed a modest 8-pointer and was as happy with it as hunters I have seen who killed bucks twice the size.

Chris spent most of the week alternating between hunting our "man-made" trails and hunting from treestands. He saw a couple of bucks that he estimated would have scored in the 140's but he stuck to his convictions about only killing a buck of a lifetime. He went home empty handed, but satisfied.

If there were a lesson here for me as a guide, it was that hunters come with a wide range of experience and woods savvy. Some are not prepared to hunt alone in the big woods of Idaho. Even the most dyed-in-the-wool buck hunter will be a little off balance. I should have started Brian off in a treestand the first morning of his hunt. Later in the week, he might have been ready to go on his own into a remote area like Bear Dog Ridge.

CHAPTER 10

The Right Equipment

When I was growing up in northern Wisconsin there was a local, legendary hunter who was known for his ability to get a big buck every fall. His name was Bob Norton and he lived alone in a small cabin just up the road from our farm. He survived by trapping beaver, muskrat, and mink and picking up an occasional odd job.

From our house, we could see the big maple tree in Bob's yard where he would hang his deer. Each November our family looked forward to watching that tree during the 9-day deer season to see just when he would have a buck hanging and how big it was. No one knew where the old man hunted or how he hunted, but whatever he did worked. Most seasons he would have one hanging by the end of the first day, some years it would take him three or four days. I don't recall a season when Bob did not get a buck. It was usually at least an 8-pointer and often one of the biggest killed by anyone in the county.

When it wasn't hunting season I would sometimes ride my bike past Bob's place and if I would see him in his yard, I would stop in to say hello. To a kid he seemed very old but as I look back, he was probably in his early 70s. Bob was cordial but a man of few words and I never got him to talk much about hunting or anything else for that matter.

Growing up in a hunting family, I was obsessed with hunting magazines and spent hours reading about guns and hunting by writers like Jack O'Connor, Russell Annabel or Elmer Keith. I also had a passion for the latest hunting equipment and newest gadgets that were written about and advertised in those magazines. Kids of all ages now have several big outdoor catalogs to satisfy their longings but in the 1950s and '60s we only had a few hunting magazines and the famed *Herter's* catalog.

I was itching to know more about the guns, scopes, and other "stuff" that old Bob used for getting those dandy bucks. Once I asked him what deer rifle he hunted with and his response was, "Just a thirty-thirty."

Another time I asked him what he thought of putting a scope on a rifle and he said, "No need for one of them. Just makes a gun hard to carry." That was the most I ever got out of Bob and I didn't press further.

One November when I was about 16 and had been hunting for a few years, I met up with Bob—actually he met up with me—in the woods. I was on a stand overlooking a finger of land where deer often crossed an old beaver flowage. I was backed up against a big Norway pine where I was sure I could see anything coming. The old man seemed to appear out of nowhere. He was standing in a thick patch of balsam trees no more than 30 feet from me. His hat was pulled down so his eyes barely peered out from under the brim. Bob was tall and thin with a slight hump to his back. He was such a part of the woods that I hadn't noticed him and had no idea how long he had been watching me. I gave him an embarrassed nod. He grinned back then ambled up to me.

I remember saying, "Hi Bob, I didn't see you right away."

He stepped closer, put his back to the same tree as if we were hunting together, spit a brown streak of snoose and whispered, "I know."

I felt even more embarrassed as I whispered back, "Guess we should be quiet. See anything today? "

Bob told me that he had killed a buck a couple of hours earlier on the other side of Slim Creek and dragged it to the road below the beaver flowage. I recall being amazed that such an old guy was still hunting alone and dragging big bucks out of the woods by himself. He was heading cross-country to get to his old Chevy pickup, which was parked about three miles away on a different road. Bob said he had spotted me from across the beaver flowage and knew I was a Skille, though he was not sure which one.

"So, how big is he?" I said, trying not to show too much excitement.

Bob gave me a slightly puzzled look and said, "Oh, I suppose he will go 180 pounds. Looks to be in pretty good shape too."

I realized then why I had never seen horns tacked up anywhere around his place like most local hunters had—he wasn't hunting for horns.

My brother and I could not resist driving by his house the next day to check out the buck. There it was, hanging from the same limb of the big maple where all the others had hung over the years. It was a beautiful non-typical with at least five long points on each beam and several odd points. The multiple brow points were dark brown and knurly.

Bob would hang his bucks for a few days, then drag them into his one-room cabin and skin, cut and wrap, and put the meat in his freezer. He would help my dad butcher hogs every fall and get half of a hog in return for the help. With a buck and about 100 pounds of pork, he was good for the year. Bob led a simple life by today's standards. His hunting success was not motivated by competition, he didn't have a bragging bone in his body and he just liked to hunt big bucks, was good at it, and needed the venison.

The day I met him in the woods he was wearing black wool pants, which had that permanent baggy-in-the-knees look, a red plaid wool coat so old you could hardly tell the red from the black squares, and a brown waterproof canvas hat. I recognized the hat as the same one he wore when he was not hunting—it was his everyday hat.

His rifle was a break-open single shot .30-30 just as plain as a rifle could be. It had no sling and no scope, just a little rear sight and a small blade front sight with a brass bead. The bluing was mostly worn off the old barrel and there was no finish left on the stock. When he walked, the rifle balanced over the crook in his arm with the buttstock under his armpit. It was hardly noticeable, as though it were a part of him. When he stood, he rested the crescent butt plate on the toe of his pack boot.

I could see a small knife in a sheath on Bob's belt. The leather handle and sheath looked as worn as the belt that held them. The pocket on his wool shirt had the unmistakable bulge from a can of chew. That was the extent of Bob's equipment; he carried nothing else but the rifle in his hand.

When I think of that day I can't help but visualize what a contrast he was to hunters I see today. But for the rifle, you wouldn't suspect that Bob was hunting. He wasn't decked out in waterproof, breathable, camouflage clothes over sweat-wicking, synthetic underwear. I doubt if he would have known the temperature rating of his worn pack boots, or cared. He definitely would have sneered at the idea of masking his scent with some spray-on chemical or locking it within his clothing, which in Bob's case would have been tough to do.

Bob had no fanny pack, daypack or any of the things we feel are necessities today. I can only imagine what old Bob would

Clothing that worked well for hunters 40 years ago works as well today. Dressed in warm and quiet wool pants, coat, and felt hat this buck hunter is comfortable on a cold, snowy November day.

have thought if he could see us pull out our GPS units, grunt tubes, rattling bags, cover scents, chemical hand warmers, cameras, field dressing kits, and Lord knows what all.

I can hear him asking, "What you gonna do with all that stuff?"

And I doubt if he would have been much impressed with our synthetic-stocked stainless steel rifles, variable scopes with range finding reticules, waterproof scope covers, fancy detachable slings, and all the other paraphernalia that go with them. Today's rifle makes and models in dozens of arousing new cartridges would have bored him. He would have been flabbergasted to know what today's hunters spend on unneccessary things. Bob would have been most interested in how we hunted and what we killed, and that's how he would have judged us. I think Bob and so many other hunters from that era knew that simple was better.

After many years of hunting and guiding I can now look back and understand why old Bob did so well. He kept his equipment to a minimum and was not bogged down with what he would call "gadgets."

Bob had the simplest of rifles — one that was easy to carry and fast to shoot. He could concentrate on hunting rather than fiddling with gear. I know little about his hunting style or his woods savvy but I'm certain that he rarely missed an opportunity at a buck because of equipment problems.

Now, I am not suggesting that we all go back to single shot thirty-thirties, throw away our scopes, and just hunt for meat. I believe strongly, however, that many of us could become better hunters simply by re-evaluating what we carry into the woods.

Each year that I guided, I experienced a hunt or two where there were major difficulties because of equipment. Many of my hunters could have taken some pointers from old Bob on keeping things simple. One hunt in particular stands out in my mind.

In 1994, I was guiding a fellow from Virginia — I will call him Warren — during the last week of November. This was his second hunt with me; he had killed a medium size 8-pointer two years earlier. On that previous hunt Warren had too much gear. He carried a large daypack with extra clothing, survival gear, and binoculars. These were the things I knew he had but I am sure there was more. I had tactfully suggested that he not carry the pack since it was heavy and made shooting difficult.

Warren was not one to take much advice from a guide, so here he was on his second hunt with the same pack full of stuff. Besides that, he had returned with a rifle and scope combination that was not good for hunting in the timber of Idaho.

I had placed him in a treestand before daylight for an early morning hunt, and was in the truck drinking coffee and killing time when I heard him shoot twice. About 10 minutes later he shot again. Finally, he came out to the truck and told me he had wounded a huge whitetail buck.

The buck had come by his stand following two does. Warren took two shots, hitting the buck high in the front left leg with the second shot. Warren tracked the deer, jumped him, and missed another shot. So, we went back in together and started to track. We had about 10 inches of snow but it was frozen and crusty, with lots of old and new deer tracks.

We tracked this buck until dark and jumped him at least four times without firing a shot. Warren kept berating himself for not having any experience shooting at running deer.

However, from my viewpoint lack of experience was minor compared to his equipment problems, the most serious of which was a variable 4½X-14X scope. Experienced or not, he wasn't able to find the running buck at close range in the scope. I had always disliked big scopes for woods hunting, and this situation was not making me love them any more.

His second problem was his rifle. He was carrying a heavy Weatherby Mark V rifle in .270 Weatherby Magnum caliber with an unwieldy barrel — I believe it was 26 inches. This was a good rifle for open country shooting, but certainly not what we needed that day.

In addition, Warren had dressed his pet rifle with a padded rifle cover. I had never seen one of these used but Warren had told me it was to protect the rifle from scratches and weather. It appeared to me that he was having trouble handling the gun with that slippery padding, especially while wearing gloves. We had to give up at dark and hope that it didn't snow during the night.

Poor Warren stayed awake and paced the floor all night. The next morning we were ready to take up the track when it was just getting light. It hadn't snowed, so blood and tracks would be easy to see. As a rule, I didn't carry a rifle while guiding but this day I took my pre-'64 Winchester Model 70 rifle in .30-'06 caliber just in case it turned out to be a long chase. This rifle was a featherweight with a 22-inch barrel and topped with a 1¾X-5X variable Redfield scope. I was accustomed to the rifle and had hunted with it for many years.

I did not tell Warren, but I had lost faith in his ability to make his rifle and scope combination work. Of course he wanted to kill his own buck if possible, and I could not blame him. It's no fun to go home and tell your buddies that the guide had to finish your deer. So, I promised that I would not shoot if Warren had any chance to kill the buck on his own.

I really hoped we would find the buck dead that morning, but in a few hundred yards we jumped him. He had bedded in the same spot all night. Warren was in front of me so he could do the shooting when the buck got up. He had plenty of time for a shot as the buck struggled stiffly to his feet. With each jump the buck gained momentum and was soon out of sight. Again, Warren was left struggling with the sling, scope covers, and safety, while we lost our first chance. Now we had this big buck up and going again.

That old deer took us on a long, tough trip back over much of the same ground we had covered the day before. We had old blood, new blood and dozens of tracks, including our own. By 10:00 A.M., we had jumped him about three more times and things were really looking grim.

Finally, the track took us up over a ridge in heavy timber and brush. As we eased over the ridge I spotted the buck bedded down in thick brush about 40 yards below us. Warren was a few feet to my left and couldn't see him. I could only see one antler and an ear and then just a faint outline of the body behind lots of brush. I tried to get Warren to step over my way so he could see the deer but he motioned for me to shoot. I got my sights on the buck and whistled to get him to stand up or move so I could have a clear shot. I whistled about four times but the buck only turned his head and would not move. At that point, I figured he was becoming weak and didn't want to get up so I took a chance and shot through the brush. He flopped over and slid a few feet down the hill. We were overjoyed to have finally ended this ordeal. We shook hands, congratulated each other, and danced around like a couple of kids with their first deer.

As we got over to the buck and looked him over more closely, Warren said, "Those horns don't look the same as I remember when I first shot him yesterday."

I replied, "Well he does look a little narrower than I expected." Jokingly I added, " This must be one of those old cases of 'ground shrinkage'."

I rolled the deer over to look at that broken left leg we had been tracking for two days, and my heart sank. No broken leg or previous wounds at all. I had shot the wrong buck!

After examining tracks and this buck's bed, it became painfully obvious what had happened. Warren's wounded buck had passed within 50 feet of this buck and continued on. This poor, unlucky buck had just bedded in the wrong place that day and I had assumed he was our wounded buck. If I could have gotten a better look at his antlers, I would have known he was a different buck. We were fairly sure Warren's buck was a big, wide 8-pointer. This buck was a 5X6 with double brow tines and not nearly as wide as Warren's. I quickly tagged and field dressed this "mistaken" 13-pointer and we continued after the wounded buck.

We jumped him once more without Warren getting off a shot. At that point we decided to split up. Warren's large daypack was beginning to weigh him down and he was getting slow and tired. I took the track and Warren stayed in a good open area where the buck had passed through a couple of times already. I felt sure that if I kept after him he would eventually run into Warren. If Warren could have time to see the deer coming, he might be able to kill it.

If a trophy hunter were to limit himself to 10-point bucks or larger,
he would find this 4X4 hard to pass up.

I tracked the buck until I could ease up on him bedded and I killed him. This time before shooting, I could see the wound and was positive that it was the right buck.

He turned out to be a very symmetrical 8-pointer with a 24-inch spread, one of the widest and biggest our hunters had ever gotten. It was an exciting day and Warren was thrilled with his buck even though he did not get a chance to make the finishing shot. I feel very lucky that we were able to get the buck; many things went wrong and we came close to losing the track several times.

I am convinced that Warren would have killed the buck himself and much earlier in the chase but two things were going against him. Much of his equipment was not suited for hunting whitetails in northern Idaho. His rifle was too heavy and long of barrel to handle well in the thick brush and timber. It was encumbered with a sling, a protective jacket, and a scope with far too much magnification for close running shots. In addition, Warren's heavy pack made traveling and fast shooting very difficult.

Secondly, Warren was not familiar with this rifle and scope set-up. He told me later that his only hunting experience with that gun was sitting on what he referred to as "green fields" in Virginia and making long deliberate shots at unsuspecting deer.

There are some uplifting aspects to this story. Warren proved to be a conscientious hunter and a safe gun handler. Also, he was willing to stick to that trail for as long as it took and he deserved the buck.

Most importantly, Warren learned from the experience. He told me afterwards that when he got home he was going to get a fanny pack and only carry as much extra equipment as he could fit in it. He called me later that winter and said he bought a new Remington semiautomatic carbine in .308 with a 2X-7X Leupold scope. He called it his "Idaho Brush Gun."

After that hunt I began a policy of sending each of my hunters a list of equipment I thought was necessary and encouraged them to keep things simple. My list included one small flashlight, a compass, matches, a small knife for field dressing, 10 cartridges, a small camera and compact binoculars and a lunch if we were to be out all day. These items could be carried in coat pockets, eliminating the need for back or fanny packs. As their guide, I could carry things for them like a drag rope, rattling antlers, extra clothes, larger binoculars, and extra food in a daypack.

I let hunters know that light, fast-handling rifles with low-power scopes are good combinations for Idaho's timber and close-range shooting. I like to think that my old friend Bob Norton would have agreed with these suggestions.

One final thought about those two days when Warren and I tracked that big buck. The hunt reinforced my conviction that whitetail guides should not carry rifles. This situation was one of the very rare times when it could be justified and even then, it got messy. Most sportsmen would agree that finishing a wounded deer for someone else is the ethical thing to do. However, there are folks who would be quick to point out that a guide, or anyone for that matter, should have a licence and tag before shooting any deer — that gives a guide only one time per season to "help out" a hunter.

We could argue forever as to whether I did the right thing. Nevertheless, when I see guides routinely carrying rifles I am convinced they are asking for problems. If I were a hunter paying a guide, I would insist that he leave his rifle at home.

My mistaken buck was not part of the plan but he was a beautiful 10-pointer with a double brow point on the right and a triple on the left. I put my tag on him and in spite of the mistake, I'll remember him as much as any I've shot.

CHAPTER 11

The Lawn Chair Buck

There never were many easy hunts. Most bucks were hard earned through hours of treestand sitting, miles of stillhunting, or dozens of attempts at rattling. Now and then, a buck would happen along with no planning on my part. The surprised hunter would make an easy shot and go home happy, never realizing that his guide had no clue as to how it happened. Those "bonus bucks" were not as satisfying from a guiding standpoint but I never complained. This story stands alone as an easy hunt that was actually planned; though it took some surprising turns before it was over.

I was guiding alone that November in 1996. My first hunters were three fellows from Mississippi. We had hot dry weather and poor hunting. We could not move in the woods without making a racket. With the warm weather, the deer seemed to move only at night. Those southern boys did not mind the heat at all; I guess they thought it was typical for November in Idaho. Only one of the three killed a buck and that was a modest 8-pointer.

The week after the Mississippi hunters went home, the weather remained warm and dry. I guided two more hunters from Pennsylvania who each killed a buck, but nothing to brag about. Conditions were tough. It was one of those seasons where the bucks didn't know the rut was on. The only good thing about the weather was that it was pleasant in the woods. We hunted in light clothing and even then it was too warm for much hiking during mid-day.

Week three finally showed a change in the hunting conditions. We got some cooler weather and a couple inches of snow.

I had three more hunters from New York and two of them killed bucks. One was a small 8-pointer and the other a very good 12-pointer that scored in the upper 150s B&C. The weather had changed, the rut had changed, and so had our luck!

Now we were in the last week of the season and it was looking to be a good one. Though the miles were wearing me down, I was looking forward to guiding three hunters from Vermont. Jesse and Greg were brothers who had been out before and this time they brought Bill, a friend of theirs and long-time hunting partner. They were all good hunters.

Jessie was the oldest of the group and the most experienced hunter. I had learned the first year I guided him and Greg that Jessie needed very little guiding. He liked hunting alone and was capable of going off into uncharted territory with a minimum of direction from me.

The first day of their hunt Jessie killed a good 10-pointer. At his request, I had sent him alone into a remote area. At dusk

This skilled hunter from Vermont made a 250-yard shot in the dim light of dusk to bag this big 10-pointer.

when he was stillhunting his way out, he spotted a buck with two does. They were in the bottom of a deep ravine about 250 yards away. It was too late to make a closer stalk and Jessie had one chance for a shot. He quickly got into a prone position, which is evidence of an experienced hunter and rifle shot. With daylight fast running out, he was able to make the difficult shot. The big buck field dressed at 200 pounds and scored over 150 B&C points.

Greg and Bill hunted for two more days without any luck. It had snowed an additional 10 inches during the week, which was ideal for stillhunting. These boys were covering a lot of ground and we were seeing plenty of rut activity and deer movement but the big bucks these guys were after were not cooperating.

On Thursday Bill's luck changed. I had placed him in a treestand at daylight and sent Greg to stillhunt alone into a nearby area. Bill and I were to join him later in the morning. At about 10:00 A.M. I made a short deer drive to Bill's stand and

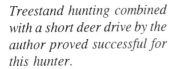

Treestand hunting combined with a short deer drive by the author proved successful for this hunter.

pushed a nice 10-point buck and doe to him. He made a great shot at the running buck and dropped him with one shot from his .308. This buck field dressed at 184 pounds.

That afternoon, as Greg and I continued hunting, the weather turned warmer and it started snowing wet heavy snow, common for November in Idaho. Melting snow hung in the trees and continually dropped on us in cold slush-balls. We hunted until dark but only managed to get wet, cold and miserable.

I had not said anything to Greg but I was concerned that the temperature might drop during the night and make hunting conditions worse. I was up at 4:00 A.M. that Friday morning to hike around camp and check the snow conditions. The thermometer read minus eight degrees Fahrenheit. The sky was clear and there was a gentle but bone-chilling breeze. As I had feared, the wet snow had frozen to a hard crust on the ground and was frozen in the trees. That put an end to stillhunting for Greg and me. I had to quickly make plans that did not involve moving in those noisy conditions.

Looking back on that day, I have to admit that I was relieved that we were forced to limit our hiking. It had been a long November and I was starting to get burned out. Though I did not admit it to my hunters, I was tired. Fortunately, Greg had done his share of hiking in deep snow that week and was anxious to try something other than stillhunting.

Greg and I were the only ones up for breakfast—Jesse and Bill were happy to sleep in and dream of their big bucks. Over breakfast we discussed our options and made plans. I pointed out to Greg that the frozen snow had made any quiet moving in the woods impossible. Our choices were down to two. I could place him in a treestand and leave him on his own for the day. Neither of us liked that option. We both knew that no place was colder than a windy treestand in Idaho's mountains when the temperature is below zero.

Our other option was to take a ground stand. I asked Greg if he would be willing to sit in one place all day if I stayed with him and guaranteed that he would be comfortable. He said he was game to try anything if I thought we had a chance of seeing a good buck.

With the increased snow depth we were becoming limited to lower elevation areas that we could reach with the truck. I knew of a ridge in a large clearcut where we could see for several hundred yards. It was just below the 3,500 feet elevation in the Gold Creek drainage so my hope was that we could drive to within a mile of the ridge. From there we could hike in to find a ground stand.

I described the place I had in mind and let Greg know that I had a reason for picking this spot. It was an area where I had seen a big buck earlier in the season. I had spooked this buck and only gotten a glimpse of him at the lower edge of the clearcut as he dove into the thick timber. As I investigated the area I had found several scrapes along the lower edge of the cut that I assumed were his.

After breakfast I quickly gathered gear for the hunt. In this case the gear consisted of plenty of sandwiches and snacks (I had asked Carolyn to pack us more than the regular), two thermoses of coffee, two wool blankets, a large daypack, and, most importantly, two comfortable lawn chairs.

Before we headed out that morning I reminded Greg to bring extra clothing because he would not be doing any hiking other than to get to the clearcut. I packed our extra clothes and our larger-than-normal lunches in my daypack.

We had left camp well before daylight and arrived at the hike-in point in the dark. Just as we were gathering our gear and ready to leave the truck, a pickup drove up. The driver, a local hunter I had known for years, stuck his head out the truck window and saw that it was me with one of my hunters. He immediately noticed the stuffed pack on my back, two blankets under one arm, two folding lawn chairs under the other arm, and a thermos in each hand. In astonishment he said, "Jeez Jack, you guys going on a picnic?"

All I could say in response was, "No, this is just the way we hunt."

I'm sure that fellow has wondered what on earth a guide and hunter were doing with all that gear, especially two lawn chairs, on a cold November morning in the mountains of Idaho.

We have run into each other since then but neither of us has brought up the subject.

Our timing was about right and we arrived at the big clearcut just as the morning was getting light. We worked our way out onto the ridge in the middle of the cut and set up our lawn chairs. Greg and I each wrapped a wool blanket around ourselves from the waste down and settled into our comfortable chairs. Our thermoses, snacks, and lunches were beside us.

The clearcut was nearly 40 acres in size and was on a steep hillside. The ridge in the middle gave us enough elevation so we could see most of the cut. The only cover in the cut was stumps, logs and a few patches of brush about 4-6 feet tall. With the snowcover it would be easy to see any deer that entered the cut from the timber. I knew this area well and from my past experience I knew that the timber surrounding this cut was good deer habitat, but very dense and difficult to hunt. Our only chance of seeing a buck was if it stepped into the open.

I mentioned to Greg that any shot he got would be a long one. The nearest timber was at least 200 yards from us and some areas of the cut were over 400 yards — too far for an easy shot. I was confident that if we sat all day we would see something.

The morning slipped by with no sign of deer. We were warm, comfortable, and well fed, however by noon we both were starting to wonder if we had made the right decision. I reminded Greg that there were no good alternatives for hunting in the deep, crunchy snow conditions and we stayed put.

At about 12:30 we heard voices and footsteps in the crunchy snow. Finally, two hunters appeared at the lower edge of the cut. Their rifles were slung over their shoulders and they were making no attempt at being sneaky. They were 250 yards away but we could hear them talking, and making enough noise to alert any deer for a half-mile. In our lawn chairs Greg and I stuck out like two penguins on an iceberg, but these guys never saw us. They continued to hunt along the bottom of the cut and out of sight. This was fouling our hunting but it convinced us that moving quietly was impossible.

In an hour the two hunters returned on their back tracks

and disappeared in the direction they had come. By 2:30 P.M. things had settled down and we continued our vigil.

All of sudden Greg, who was sitting in his chair to the right of me, sprang to his feet, threw up his rifle and fired a shot. At the shot, his aluminum chair went flying and Greg lost his footing and fell to one knee. He was up in an instant and continued shooting. I got my binoculars focused on the ant-sized deer that Greg was flinging lead at. I could see that a buck had stepped out of the timber onto the old logging road where the hunters had hiked less than an hour earlier. The distance was close to 300 yards and I suggested that Greg try a sitting position to get a more steady shot. It was definitely too far to be shooting off-hand.

But, he was caught up in the heat of the moment and not listening to advice. The buck was far enough away that the sound of the rifle confused the buck more than it frightened him. He took a few steps one way then the rifle cracked and the buck turned and took a few steps in another direction. Greg was shooting and working that bolt like he was at the OK Corral facing the Earp brothers.

On the fourth or fifth shot the buck went down like he had been poleaxed. Greg was as surprised as he was happy. We were both overjoyed and I complemented Greg with "Great shot, Greg," though something told me to be cautious. I had learned from a couple of similar experiences that when a deer dropped instantly it could get up just as quickly. I had seen many deer hit and those that made a fast dash then piled up were likely down to stay.

However, I kept my thoughts to myself and we started down to the buck. The hillside was steep and slippery and it took us a few minutes to descend to the road. I took a different route than Greg and I reached the buck before he did. I recall that Greg stopped about 30 feet from the buck, opened the action on his rifle, unloaded it (it may have been empty from the shooting), then leaned it against a tree at the side of the old road. I was standing a few feet from the buck trying to see where the bullet had struck him. I couldn't see a bullet hole or blood, just a little hair scattered out on the snow. As Greg was approaching, I saw

Crunchy snow conditions forced an all day sit-and-watch hunt that worked for this whitetail hunter from Vermont.

the buck's eyes blink. I quickly said, "Greg, grab your rifle and load it. This buck is not dead!"

I was astonished when Greg replied, "Here, I'll just break his neck." With that he grabbed that big set of antlers, one in each hand like handlebars on a bike, and proceeded to twist the buck's neck.

Greg was a tough, young man of about 160 pounds, in good shape and in his prime. However, as anyone who has ever tried to twist a deer's head off when butchering it can tell you, it is not easy. The old buck was in the rut and had a neck like a bull moose; no man alive was about to break this buck's neck with his bare hands.

Greg twisted one way then the other. With each twist the buck's eyes opened more and life began returning. By about the third twist the buck got his feet under him and the shoving match began. Greg was no longer trying to break a neck; he was now in the self-defense mode and hanging on for survival.

I stood there dumbfounded. The ammunition for Greg's rifle was in his pocket. Greg could not let go of this much-alive buck to dig for cartridges. I glanced around for a club, rock, or anything to help end this situation that was quickly becoming desperate. There was no question that the big buck with eyes rolling and nostrils flared was getting the best of Greg.

I thought of my sheathed hunting knife on my belt. Pulling it out, I quickly plunged it into the buck's ribs at about the middle of the lungs. This was new to me and I had no idea how effective it might be, what resistance I would get, or how the buck might react. I can tell you for certain that the buck felt it. He flew into a frenzy that tested Greg's strength to the limit. Now we saw the first evidence of blood from the buck. Greg was about at the end of his wrestling endurance as the buck slowly expired.

It was a moment of mixed feelings. We were both happy to have a good buck and Greg was relieved to have the situation over and to be in one piece. He later told me that his game plan had quickly gone from breaking the buck's neck, to preventing it from getting away, and finally to keeping the buck from goring him. As a guide I was relieved that neither of us got hurt and glad there were no witnesses.

As we examined the buck it became apparent that Greg's last shot had grazed the buck behind the base of the antlers. The .270 bullet had cut a half-inch furrow of hide and hair and only nicked the buck's skull. If the shot would have been a fourth of an inch lower the hunt would have ended easily, that much higher and we may never have seen the buck again.

Greg and I relearned something we already knew, that long-range off-hand shots are very iffy at best. Jack O'Connor's old advice would have helped Greg that day. He once wrote, "Never shoot off-hand if you can take a rest. Never shoot standing if you can kneel. Never kneel if you can sit. And never sit if you can shoot from a prone position." Will Greg ever take a long off-hand shot again? Not if there is any way he can rest the rifle or get into a more steady position.

I have always harped that there is no easy way to get big bucks and that we have to work for them. This hunt started out easy. After all, we spent most of that day sitting in lawn chairs sipping coffee and eating cookies. We planned not to work hard for this one. In the end, the Lawn Chair Buck was anything but easy. Maybe my harping was right after all.

CHAPTER 12

Letters from Hunters

Viewed from the outside, one might think guiding is all about traipsing through the woods with hunters, telling stories, photographing hunters with their big bucks, and generally being cool and macho. But, like any business, there is much behind-the-scenes work. A lot of time is spent on the paperwork of advertising, insurance, taxes, licenses, and permits. There are hunting licenses to buy, guides to hire, and vehicles and gear to maintain. Scouting, treestand placement, and opening hunting trails — things that a hunter might consider fun — become work in a guiding business. One of the most time consuming jobs for a guide is answering inquiries from potential hunters.

Initially, I tried different ways to advertise my new guiding business. I rented booth space at sportsmen shows where I could meet potential hunters face-to-face. This is a very popular method for many outfitters and I booked many of my early clients this way. However, I found that placing ads in hunting magazines reached a larger audience and brought more contacts without the expense and travel that shows required.

Deer and Deer Hunting magazine proved to be the best advertising publication for me. It was a magazine specifically aimed at whitetail deer hunters, had a big circulation in the East and Mid-west and was relatively inexpensive. I could place a medium size ad with a black and white photo for about $300 per issue, a little cheaper per issue if I had it run for several months.

In the early years, sportsmen shows helped the author to contact hundreds of hunters and book many of his first clients. The hat seemed necessary for a western outfitter!

As those magazine ads hit the news stands and were mailed to subscribers I started getting inquiries from dozens of hunters. I made it a policy to answer every letter and do my best to give honest answers even when the answers might turn the client away. For example, it was tough to answer questions like "Do you guarantee success?", "How many Boone and Crockett bucks have you taken?", and "About how many trophy bucks can I expect to see in a 6-day hunt?" The honest answers to those questions were "no, one, and very few — maybe none."

I found myself writing fairly long replies that were often a short version of Basic Whitetail Hunting. I would explain that it is very difficult to guarantee anything in the business of guiding. There are so many things that are out of my control, such as hunter ability, weather, and just plain luck.

To answer the "How many B&C bucks?" question I would describe that thousands of trophy bucks are killed every year across the country and that very few meet the strict antler length, mass, and symmetry requirements of B&C. As to the "How many trophy bucks?" question, I had to honestly answer "very few." I would explain that many of my hunters killed the first buck they saw (this was often the first deer they had seen!) and, in many cases, it was the biggest buck they had ever killed. These were certainly trophy bucks to the hunters taking them but few were anywhere near record book bucks.

The great majority of hunters asked good questions and had reasonable concerns about what they were getting into. The most common questions were about numbers of hunters in camp, sleeping and eating accommodations, required gear, type of terrain and weather they would be hunting in, and how we hunted whitetails in Idaho.

Of the hundreds of letters I received, I have included a few that give insight into the thinking of some of our fellow hunters. Some are exactly as they were written. Others are my paraphrased recollection of letters. All are true. Most of them are good examples of "How not to write to a guide." I have avoided using real names.

Dear Sirs:

My name is Todd and I am from New York. I'm 14 years old and last year I killed my first buck alone, with my dad. He was a nice one. This year I didn't do too good. We had no snow so I guess tracking was not good and stuff. The reason I am writing is because all my life I have wanted to get a big buck—the kind my uncles call "farm bucks" back here. I thought if I came out west where not many hunters are I could get a big one. I have no money but I am a handy kid to have around. Could I split wood, carry water, skin deer and stuff around camp for maybe a free hunt? Please let me know soon since I am sending this letter to other guides and plan to take the first good offer offered to me.

Thank You,
Todd S.
Potsdam, NY

Every year I got at least a couple of letters from guys inquiring about working as a guide. This was the only letter asking to hunt in trade for work. I saved this kid's letter because I loved his honesty and self-confidence, even if he was a little naïve. I hope he eventually got an offer to head west on a big buck hunt.

Dear Jack,

How y'all doing up there in Idaho? Good I hope. I am writing to let you know that B. J. Renton, Bobby Ray Farmington, and myself are all looking forward to our hunt with y'all the end of October. The 3 of us are good old boys and best friends and all work together at Mississippi Plywood. However, we really have not hunted together much — only for a day or two for boar pigs here in Miss. and one little old hunt in South Miss. for quail.

Without bragging I wanted to let you know before we got there that I'm the most experienced hunter of the 3 of us. With that sure-enough fact in mind would you give some thought to finding some remote parts of y'all's guiding area that do not get hunted and where the chances are better for an exceptional big old buck? When the boys and I hunt with you I would be willing to go alone with some guidance from you into those areas. I am a good woods-man with swamp savvy and don't need a guide all that much. If you can do this for me and if I killed a really good hog-buck I would shore enough make it worth your while moneywise? You can let me know when we get there to Idaho.

Your (soon-to-be) Mississippi friend,
Buddy T.
Houlka, MS

This was an example of the type of hunter who guides try to avoid. He was more concerned about himself than his partners and he was a little arrogant. His offer to "make it worth my while" told me he did not understand how guides operate. Most guides want their hunters to be successful — extra money will not intice them to do more for the hunter.

Dear Mr. Skille,

Thank you for sending me your hunting brochure. I am a professional baseball player — outfielder for the Pittsburgh Pirates — maybe you recognize my name? My friend Bill H. is a member of the Pirates also — Bill plays first base. I have enclosed our autographed photos and a couple of our signed baseball cards. I hope you enjoy these. We would like to book a hunt with you this coming November and are wondering if you could give us free hunts. We would be more than happy to let you use our names to endorse your guiding business. Also, if we had a successful hunt I know other baseball players from several big league teams who are hunters and would likely book your services in the future. Please give this offer some thought and let me know what we can work out.

Steve G.
Pittsburgh, PA

There was probably nothing wrong in using this approach to get a free hunt. I was not a baseball fan so it didn't work with me. Making a connection between the sports of hunting and baseball seemed a little presumptious to me. I wondered what he would have thought if I had written to him and asked for free tickets to a game because I was a well known whitetail hunter?

Dear Jack,

I enjoyed talking with you on the phone and I got your letter confirming our hunt for this November. After our conversation I got to thinking of some questions and concerns maybe you can answer. First of all I'm not sure which gun to bring. I have quite a collection but have boiled it down to my favorite pre-'64 Model 70 Winchester in .300 H&H Magnum. You said that many deer are shot there at less than 100 yards but sometimes they are shot at long distances across clearcuts—maybe 300 yards or so? My plan is to load 200 gr. round nose bullets for close range, 180 gr. spire points for medium range, and 150 gr. spire points for anything over 200 yards. This way I can load one of the heavy bullets in the chamber, two medium weight bullets in the top of the magazine, and have the flatter shooting 150 gr. rounds in the bottom of the magazine. When we jump a deer at close range I'll shoot the heavy brush-bucking bullet first and by the time he is out there a ways I'll have the faster stepping ones ready to go.

My second question — you mentioned that your cabins are heated with wood stoves. I am very concerned, as is Art, that the wood smoke will impregnate our clothes and deer will be alerted by this. If possible could we stay in a motel nearby and you or one of your guides pick us up each morning?

My third and last question — I've been reviewing the *Farmer's Almanac* for moon phases and I see that the 2nd week of November (the week we booked) is right in the full moon phase. I am concerned that deer movements will be at night and daytime hunting will be poor. Could Art and I switch to the previous or the following week to avoid this? If so, which of those two weeks do you recommend?

Please let me know your thoughts about these issues.

Ronald O.
New London, Wisconsin

Besides sending this letter, this hunter called several times before his hunt with more concerns. He had a way of turning hunting into work for himself as well as his guide. Every plan I came up with was questioned and analyzed to death. On his fifth day of hunting he killed a good 8-pointer that scored about 140 B&C. His first comment was, "If this buck only had another point on each side and two inches more on each point he would make 160." I never asked which bullet he was using when he killed the deer!

Idaho Whitetail Guides:

I am a trophy hunter of the first order. I don't settle for just any buck but I'm willing to pay extra to a guide who can put me onto a B&C whitetail. If you know of a booney in your area and are reasonably sure you could get me a shot at him I would be interested in booking a hunt with you. To give you an idea of my standards I have been pursuing large mule deer for several seasons in Wyoming and Colorado. I won't settle for less than a 40 inch muley. Please respond at your earliest conveinience.

Fred S.
San Diego, CA

This was only one example of many letters I received from hunters asking if I knew of a B&C buck in my hunting area. Maybe it was a legitimate question but I always interpreted it as coming from a hunter who was not knowledgeable about whitetail bucks or human nature. B&C bucks are extemely rare and difficult to measure "on-the-hoof." They are also extemely valuable — worth a lot more than what I charged for a hunt. If I somehow had been able to size-up a buck and determined he would "make the book," I would have been the first to go after him for my own trophy wall.

Dear Mr. Skille:

I'm writing to ask a different sort of question you probably haven't been asked before. I got your name from a fellow (I can't recall his name) I met at a sportsman show in Boise and he said you have lots of whitetail antlers — mounted and otherwise. I am looking to purchase a 10-point rack that scores around 140-150 B&C points. It must be a very typical rack with no odd points, not too heavy in mass, with roughly an 18-inch inside spread.

Here is the reason I need a rack like this. Last fall I was hunting with an outfitter in the Salmon River area of Idaho and I killed a buck of that description. I was actually helping the outfitter by guiding a couple hunters for him. To make a long story short, we saw this buck across a canyon around 300 yards away. One of the hunters shot at the deer just as I shot. When we got over to the dead buck it was plain that I had killed it, not him. The buck had one shot through the lungs with a very large exit hole. I shoot a .300 Win. Mag. and this client, a young fellow who had little experience, was shooting a .30-'06. With such a large exit hole it was clear that the buck was mine. However, him being a paying client and all, I had to give him the buck.

So, I would like to place a head on my wall to represent that buck. Please let me know if you have a head like that either mounted or just the horns. If you do, send me pictures and your asking price. I am willing to pay a good fair price.

Len S.
Boise, ID

I did have a couple of sets of antlers that would have fit his description but I didn't write back to him. His letter left a bad taste in my mouth. It reminded me of the spoiled kid who lost the tennis match but felt he should have won, so he asked Dad to buy him a trophy to prove that he had won after all.

Dear Whitetail Guides:

I am planning to book a whitetail hunt for this November. I am not a trophy hunter and I have never hunted whitetail deer before. On my den wall I have a nice 4X4 mule deer, and a pretty good 14 ½ inch antelope I got in Wyoming last year. I also have a pretty fair 3X3 blacktail I got in Oregon in 1995. I now need a whitetail buck, nothing huge, just a representative head with 5 or 6 points to a side and a modest spread of around 22 inches. Do you have this size bucks in your area? Can you guarrantee me a buck like that? I don't mean guarrantee to get one, just a shot at one. I am fairly easy to please.

> Ted N.
> Ogden, Utah

This letter struck me as coming from a hunter who was planning a shopping trip to the mall rather than a hunting trip. The fenced-in whitetail hunts that are becoming popular are ready-made for this type of hunter. I wrote back to him explaining that a 10 or 12-point whitetail with a 22 inch spread is a very big buck and would not be easy to get. I never heard from him again.

Dear Idaho Whitetail Guides:

Do you have any openings for a 3-4 day one-on-one guided whitetail hunt during the last week of October? I will tell you up-front that I am not interested in pretty scenery or a fun experience in the woods. I want to kill a buck as quickly as possible, then move on. My hunting goal is to kill a legal whitetail buck in every state that has a season on them. I may be the first to do this. This year I have hunts booked in Arizona, Wyoming, S. Dakota, and Kansas. I would also like to squeeze in an Idaho hunt. I am traveling with a pickup and camper so I don't need lodging accommodations. Also,

if I book a hunt and kill a buck the first day I assume I won't
be paying for the remaining days. Let me know ASAP if you
have an opening.

> Ward B.
> Denver, CO

I was foolish enough to book this guy for a 4-day hunt in
1988. He stuck to his convictions—he was not happy with the
scenery and had no fun in the woods. I was the only one who
had less fun. He was a very inexperienced hunter, was poorly
equipped, and worst of all he would absolutely not take advice
or direction. By the first afternoon he was telling me where and
how we should hunt. He didn't kill a buck and I never heard if
he reached his goal.

Dear Sir:

I would like to send my husband on a hunting trip for
Christmas, I may even consider coming with him. Could you
send me a brochure containing the information and a price
list? He is mainly interested in a wild hog and whitetail
buck combination hunt.

With me being a resident of Georgia, I need to know if
your state requires us to have an out of state license. If we
need them could you tell me how much they would be and
how I could go about purchasing them.
Sincerely Yours,

> Mary N.
> Strouse, GA

This was not an outlandish letter but was much more common than I would have guessed before I got into the guiding
business. I received many like it asking about hunting whitetail
and antelope, whitetail and muledeer, whitetail and elk, and
several other combinations. It helped me to be more understand-
ing of these letters if I imagined myself planning an African sa-
fari. I might inquire about hunting kudu and rhino on the same
hunt. For all I know, there is not a kudu within 500 miles of a
rhino anywhere in Africa.

Gentlemen:

Could you please send me information on your whitetail hunts? Could you tell me how many 170+ B&C bucks you have taken in the past ten years? Gross and net scores?

Yours Truly,

Curt S.
Blaine, MN

It was inevitable that if I answered this question with the truth — we only killed one buck that scored over 170 — this hunter would book with a different outfitter. It reminded me of the classic question "Are you still beating your wife?" There was no honest answer that could make me look good. This hunter was a prime target for a dishonest guide who would give him the answers he was hoping for.

Dear Sirs:

I am writing to you because I am looking to book a hunt for whitetail deer this fall. I have several questions that will help me narrow my choice of outfitters. This letter will be going out to many outfitters in both the U.S. and Canada.

1. What is the cost of your hunt and what is included for that price?
2. Is the hunt for 5 or 6 days?
3. If you offer guide service, what is the cost for the week, and how do the guides work with the hunters?
4. Are your accommodations cabins, lodges, or tent camps?
5. What has your success rate been for the last few years?
6. What size deer have your clients taken on the average?
7. What type of terrain do you hunt?
8. Could you send photos of your average bucks?
9. What is the length of shots I may expect to take?
10. What type of hunting proves to be the most successful for you, stalking, drives or use of treestands?
11. If you hunt from treestands, would a large person like myself present a problem?
12. Will I be able to purchase my hunting license through you and how much is the cost?
13. If I have to fly to your destination, can arrangements be made for pick up at the nearest airport?

14. What month, and week would you recommend for my best success?
15. What type of weather could I expect then?

I would like to thank you for your time and any additional information you can add.

Sincerely,
Roger D.
Ames, Iowa

For an initial inquiry letter this was far too detailed. No guide can afford to spend the time it would take to answer all those questions. People who wrote letters like this only got my brochure and price list. Most of the time they never wrote back. My guess is these were not serious inquiries — only guys who were dreaming about going on a guided hunt.

CHAPTER 13

Is a Guided Hunt for You?

Going on a whitetail hunt away from home can be a terrific experience or it can be a nightmare; it all depends on the planning you put into it plus a degree of luck. Your first decisions will involve picking a place to go. This usually depends on what you have read, heard from other hunters, or seen on TV and videos. It also depends on how far you want to travel and the kinds of conditions you want to hunt under. For example, in the prairie states and some Canadian provinces, you will hunt whitetails in open, flat country. In Canada you may be limited to treestand hunting in very cold weather. In contrast, if you hunt in Idaho or Montana you can expect steep hills, deep canyons, and dense timber. In many parts of the Midwest, you will be limited to stand hunting in agricultural land. In Texas you can expect hot weather and baited deer on big private ranches.

Your second decision will be whether to go with a guide or to go on your own. If you are an experienced hunter, then a do-it-yourself whitetail hunt is a reasonable option. You don't need someone to haul you and your gear back into the mountains like you would on an elk hunt. Deer are a manageable size for field dressing, dragging, and meat processing. With some scouting you should not have much trouble recognizing deer habitat, finding their trails, and even locating scrapes and rubs. If you have hunted deer with some success back home, these same tactics will get you started.

There are, however, several good reasons to choose a guided

hunt over a do-it-yourself hunt. On a guided hunt you won't use up your time scouting for deer sign and figuring out how to hunt them. A guide will get you into the good spots immediately.

One of the most important things a guide offers is the peace of mind that comes with knowing you are hunting on land that is open to hunting. A few years ago I went on a mule deer hunt in Wyoming with a friend. We thought we had done our homework and knew roughly where we would hunt. Our plan was to hunt eastern foothills a few miles west of Big Piney. Our maps indicated the area had federal land, which is usually open to hunting.

We drove over a thousand miles to get to Big Piney, got a motel, and found a couple of restaurants. The next morning with map in hand we headed out to hunt. To our surprise, we started running into gated roads and "No Hunting" signs. There was plenty of federal land open to hunting but it was bordered by private ranch land, which was closed to hunting. Many of the roads had deep ruts and washouts and were not driveable. We spent the first day driving, reading the map, knocking on ranch doors, and trying to determine private from public land.

The rest of the week wasn't much better. We could never relax and enjoy the hunt. Every time we would see a pickup truck we would wonder if we had gotten onto private land and were about to get a verbal beating or worse. I managed to kill a modest 4X4 buck on that hunt but I can't say I enjoyed the experience.

If time is not a factor and you are a person who feels comfortable asking for permission and can spit and whittle with landowners, then a do-it-yourself hunt may be fine. Once you have made the contacts and learned how to hunt an area, you have a hunt you can plan on year after year.

If you decide that a guided hunt is best for you, the trick is to pick the right guide offering hunts in the state or province you have chosen. When you start looking, you may find the terms "guide" and "outfitter" to be confusing. Although many hunters—including outdoor writers—use these terms interchangeably, they are not necessarily the same, at least in many western states.

*Guided hunts can provide the unexpected bonuses of
camp comaraderie and lasting friendships.*

In Idaho, for example, it is the outfitter who is assigned a specific area to conduct a guiding business and he holds an outfitter license. Montana, Wyoming and Colorado have similar licensing requirements. Only the outfitter can advertise, book hunters, and charge fees. Guides must work under licensed outfitters and cannot contract with hunters for fees. If you sign up for a hunt with a guide instead of an outfitter, you have little legal recourse if the hunt goes bad. Outfitters in these western states are required to be bonded, carry liability insurance, and have documented proof that they have permission to operate on federal, state, or private land.

Throughout the rest of the country you will not see the term "outfitter" used as often and generally you will be dealing with guides when you book a hunt. You can find out guide and outfitter licensing requirements by contacting the game departments or the outfitter and guide regulating agencies in the state or province where you are planning to hunt. When you first contact a guiding business, it is advisable to ask if they hold the required licenses for guiding in that particular state or province. Most legitimate businesses will be happy to send you photocopies of their guide or outfitter licenses.

It used to be that a search for hunting guides was limited to the "Where To Go" sections in the backs of hunting magazines. However, these days the Internet is a great source. Just use one of the many search engines and look for *Kansas Whitetail Deer Guides,* for example. You will soon have a list of web sites offering guided hunts throughout the state. For a list of Idaho guides, the Idaho Outfitters and Guides Association Web site www.ioga.org, will get you started. Most western states have similar organizations.

Once you begin a search, the number of guiding operations will quickly overwhelm you. You need to pick a few of interest and move on. I suggest choosing about three locations of interest, say a state in the Mid-west, a western state, and one Canadian province. A reasonable number of guides to contact in each location would be four or five. If you already know which area you want to hunt then contact eight or ten guides from there. If you try the "shotgun" approach by trying to contact dozens of guides, the decision will quickly become mind boggling.

When you have your contact list boiled down, you are ready to actually start contacting guides—the fun part. This stage is too early for phone calls so just send a letter or e-mail as your first inquiry. Give a brief description of what you are interested in, i.e. whitetail hunting, with rifle or bow, number of hunters in your party, etc. You can also ask about accommodations, prices, and generally, how the guide conducts hunts.

Keep in mind this is the guide's first impression of you so don't ask questions like, "Can you guarantee me a record book buck?" If that's what you really want and you have the money you should be contacting game farms that can give you those guarantees. Be honest with yourself.

Avoid giving the impression that you are doing a mass mailing to dozens of guides, even if you are. In my business I tried to respond to everyone but if I were busy, the "to whom it may concern" letters were at the bottom of my list. Everyone likes to think he is important and form letters don't give that feeling.

As a follow-up to your initial contact, the guide will send you a brochure or point you to a Web site describing what he offers and listing prices. Some may write a letter or e-mail with more detailed answers to your questions, but don't count on it. Most guides get dozens of inquiries that go nowhere and they just can't spend much time on initial responses.

After you get the brochures or have looked over Web sites then narrow down your choices to two or three. Write back with a letter or e-mail expressing further interest. This is the time to ask specific questions like:

- What is your success rate?
- Can you send names of hunters as references?
- Can you send photos of last year's kills?
- What are advantages of early vs. late season hunts?
- What is included in the price — number of meals, lodging, care of trophy and meat, trophy fees, etc?
- How many hunters will be in camp?
- Number of hunters per guide?

A good approach is to end this letter by writing that you will be calling in a few days to discuss these questions. This saves the guide the job of writing back to you; most of these folks are not in the business because they love paperwork.

Wall-tents housed hunters in the first few years of the guiding business. They were adequate but difficult to keep warm in late November.

Keep in mind that from here on you are being judged by the guide as much as you are judging him. Everything you say or ask will add to his impression of you. You will be depending on this guy and he can give you a good hunt or he can stick you in a treestand where he knows you will not see a deer if you stay there forty days and forty nights.

Probably, the question I was most frequently asked was "How big a buck can I expect to kill?" This is a reasonable question, but one of the toughest a guide can be asked. It really puts him on the spot. He has no idea about your abilities, what the weather will be, or even what the deer population will be when you arrive. Most hunts these days are booked at least several months in advance, some a couple of years in advance. The guide will not be impressed if you describe the kind of buck you want by saying, "I'd like at least a 10-pointer with a spread of 20 inches and a B&C score of 150 or more." That tells the guide that you are not a hunter but rather a shopper and you cannot blame him if he tells you to go shop elsewhere.

Above all, do not ask him to send you maps or specific directions about where you will be hunting. This throws up a red flag that says, "I'm trying to gather enough information so my buddies and I can come there and hunt on our own." This is a dilemma that has plagued guides since the first caveman told another caveman about a favorite hunting spot. Guides do not like to give out detailed hunt information, so don't ask for it. This applies to any stage in your communications, even after your hunt.

The same goes for hunters who book a hunt one year, learn the area and methods, then return on their own in following years to hunt without the guide. Hunters justify the practice with, "Well, it is public land open to everyone," "It is leased ground and I can pay the landowner myself," or "I'm not breaking any laws." It has always baffled me that a person who would feel embarrassed to ask an auto mechanic if he can watch the mechanic work so he can do it himself next time doesn't hesitate to ask a guide about the possibilities of hunting on his own next year. As a guide, I resigned myself to the fact that there

*Jack and Carolyn Skille standing in front of one of their log cabins
used in their later years of guiding—a big improvement over tents.*

was not much I could do if a hunter returned and hunted my
area. However, I view the practice as unethical, right up there
with selling life insurance to little, old ladies.

A final temptation to avoid is sending photos of your trophies to a prospective guide. We are all proud of our hunting
accomplishments but there are no good reasons for your guide
to see them. He is likely to interpret the gesture as boasting and
may peg you as a blowhard. If your trophies are exceptional,
you run the risk of giving him the impression that you will be
difficult to please. After you have hunted with a guide and have
become friends then sharing your hunts and photos is fine.

By now you have spoken with two or three guides and gotten
answers to your questions. It's time to sit down with your hunting
partner(s) and pick a guide. Up to this point in your phone conversations you have heard several good things and may have heard a
few things that may be causing you to hesitate.

If you have heard outlandish promises or guarantees, be careful. When I first got into the business I asked an old established

outfitter who took dozens of hunters each year how far he went in "talking up" the hunt. He said, "I tell 'em anything they want to hear to get 'em to book a hunt."

In astonishment I asked, "What happens when the hunt doesn't go the way you promised?"

He laughed and said, "Well then to hell with them. There will be a new batch of suckers signing up next year."

Your best bet for avoiding a guide with that attitude is to make use of references. If a guide refuses to give references, drop him like a hot potato. Obviously, a guide will give you names of satisfied clients, or clients he thinks were satisfied. To use these references to your best advantage you must talk to them on the phone. If there are serious faults with the guide or his operation, they will come out in a phone visit, even if the reference had a successful hunt.

I recall getting one letter asking if I could send names of satisfied as well as dissatisfied clients. This guy really wanted to cover his bases. This approach borders on being unreasonable. It didn't work with me and I doubt it would with many guides. I sent him my usual list of references. By the way, guides get permission, or should, from hunters before using them as references.

In addition to references, hunter success rates can give you some idea of how good the hunting is in an area. Not all guides will give you those data but it is worth asking. Keep in mind that each guide has a different definition of success. One might claim success if a hunter had a chance at a deer whether he wanted the deer or not. Another might claim success if a hunter had a chance at a deer he wanted to kill but couldn't. My hunter success hovered around 65 percent. Using my criteria, that meant that six to seven out of 10 hunters actually killed deer. The guy who passed up bucks and went home empty handed did not help my success rate. However, it included the spikes and fork horns that impatient hunters could not pass up. The point is, you need to ask what criteria a prospective guide uses in calculating his rate of success.

Brochures showing photographs of kills are fun to look at

but tell you very little. Guides usually show the best bucks they have taken, even if it took 20 years to collect them. Recent photos, especially from the previous year, give a better idea but keep in mind that guides seldom send photos of little bucks. If a guide is very up-front with you, he will not hesitate to provide photos of all bucks taken the previous year. That was my policy and it worked well for me. It gave hunters a feel for the range of bucks taken and if a hunter killed a modest buck, his feelings weren't hurt by my not including his buck in the next brochure. I did not send photos of the few does taken; there seemed to be no point in doing that.

You have asked all the questions, talked with references, and processed all the information and you have, finally, booked a hunt. It is November and you are waiting at some tiny, out-of-the-way airport for the guide to pick you up. (My hunters always got a kick out of the control tower at our local Idaho airport; it amounted to an airport employee standing alongside the runway with a flashlight.) You are committed, there is no turning back, and all you can do is hope you picked the right place and the right guide.

Actually, you can do more than hope. Your attitude and how you handle the next six or seven days will make a big difference in how the hunt goes.

Here I am reminded of two hunters I picked up at the airport one fall. Matt and Tom, from Michigan, were on their first guided hunt and their first trip out west. They were young and inexperienced but seemed like nice enough guys. Tom struck me right off as being overly worried about how the hunt would go. He had questions about how many bucks the previous week's hunters had gotten and if he and Matt had picked the best week. He was concerned about the weather and how bad hunting was going to be without snow.

On the 30-mile trip from the airport to our hunting camp Matt didn't say much. As Tom continued with the questions, I hoped that he was wound up over the hunt and would eventually relax. One question that puzzled me was, "Do you guide in Cat Spur Creek near the town of Bovill?" I told him that I was familiar with Cat Spur Creek, had hunted elk there a couple of times, but that it wasn't in my whitetail guiding area. Tom went on to explain that while he and Matt were waiting at the airport they met a local fellow and started talking about hunting. This stranger had hunted in Cat Spur Creek a few days earlier and related that he saw several deer and a couple of monster bucks. According to Tom, his exact words were, "You should get your guide to take you there. Those bucks were awesome." I suspected that I had not heard the last of Cat Spur Creek and the big bucks.

By about the middle of the week Matt had killed an 8-pointer. It wasn't big, but it was the best he had ever killed and he was very happy with it. Tom had passed up two or three small bucks. He had seen one big 10-pointer from a treestand but wasn't able to get a shot. He had settled down some but never seemed to be satisfied. He would not sit in the same stand more than once, even where he had seen the big buck. We could never leave one place and go to a new area soon enough to please him.

The fifth morning, as Tom and I were rolling out of camp the question I was expecting finally came: "How about going to that Cat Spur Creek where those big bucks are?" I was surprised that he was able to hold off from asking for that long. I had to tell him that it was absolutely out of the question, since I was not licensed to guide there. Besides, we had 460 square miles of licensed area to hunt in, land every bit as good as Cat Spur Creek. I know it didn't satisfy him but he never mentioned it again. My guess is that he thinks about Cat Spur Creek and those monster bucks to this day.

My point with this story is that when you pay several hundred dollars and go through the screening process to hire a guide, put your faith in him and let him guide you. In this case, Tom was willing to put his hopes on the advice of a stranger he had met for a few minutes at an airport. For all he knew the guy was totally full of hot air.

While on the guided hunt, be courteous, complimentary, considerate, and throw in a little humility. It is of no importance to the guide if you are a doctor, lawyer, bank president, or the

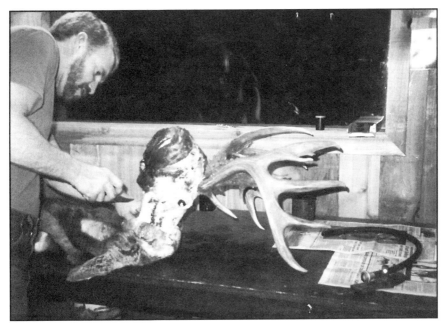

Good guiding operations provide the little extras such as caping trophies—something hunters should not have to do.

fellow who cleans their offices. The deer won't know the difference and the guide could not care less. He will judge you on how you can hunt, take direction, and primarily whether or not you are a good guy to be with.

You will unquestionably do yourself a disservice by complaining, being demanding, or being a difficult person. I am reminded here of the arrogant cuss we have all seen in a restaurant giving the waitress hell about his cold soup. He demands to talk to the cook, huffs and puffs, and creates a scene that makes all the customers uneasy. Of course, he gets an apology from the waitress and gets his soup heated. It never occurs to this guy that the apology is phony and God only knows what might be happening to his soup while it's being re-heated.

If you treat people badly, you might suffer for it. If you give a guide reason to make you suffer, you could be in for a very difficult hunt. At the end of the hunt he will shake your hand, smile, and say, "Glad you could hunt with us, it's been fun." When you call to book another hunt, he will never have an opening.

Above all else, let your guide do the guiding. You may be a great whitetail hunter back home but on a guided hunt you will be in strange country. Success, most likely, will mean doing things a little differently. Even if the guide's methods seem strange, try them. It is okay to ask questions and to make tactful suggestions. After all, I got my first lessons in rattling bucks from two of my hunters and I was grateful to them. However, don't take over.

One year I guided a fellow from Utah who had never hunted whitetails before. He had killed several big mule deer in the open country of Utah but had no experience hunting in timber like we have here in Idaho. By the end of the first day he was unhappy with the way we were hunting. Driving out of the mountains toward camp, we passed a large meadow along a creek bottom. He was beside himself with excitement and said; "Now that's where we should be hunting. In the morning we can park the truck here and just watch that meadow for deer." He was seeing a little bit of Utah in that meadow and could not resist taking over as guide. I tried to explain that whitetail here generally don't like to cross large openings like that and prefer to stick to the cover. I went on to say that in the 20 years I have hunted the area I had never seen a deer cross that meadow.

He would have no part of my opinions so the next morning there we were at daylight watching the meadow. Sitting in the truck drinking coffee was easy guiding but as I expected, we saw nothing. By noon he was becoming less thrilled with the spot and suggested we move on. The rest of the week he questioned all of my plans and insisted that we hunt his way. He never allowed himself to adapt to hunting in the timber where the deer were and did not kill a buck that week.

If you follow these suggestions, hopefully you will have a great hunt with a good guide. Keep in mind that you can still consider your hunt successful even if you don't kill a buck. Do not make the mistake of talking up the hunt to your friends before leaving for your guided hunt. This can put unnecessary pressure on you to come home with a trophy. It is better to focus on having a great experience in new country, learning different hunting methods, and making friends — including the guide. If you do get a good buck, it should be considered a bonus.

What if the hunt ends and you feel deceived and cheated out of your money and your experience. For example, if advertisements or brochures described treestands as one of the hunting methods but the guide never got around to putting up stands; you were promised one guide for every two hunters but he sent out three or four hunters with a guide. Or you found out he was not actually licensed as an outfitter or a guide where licenses are legally required. These are legitimate complaints and can be proven.

Maybe the operation was just plain slipshod. For instance, the guides were late in getting up, drank booze excessively, or were not qualified to guide hunters. The vehicles were old and unreliable, tree stands were poorly made and unsafe, and the food was below par. These are subjective complaints that fall into the category of one person's opinion verses another's.

In either case, you might have some recourse. First, you should talk to whoever is in charge as soon as there are problems. If the problems are not taken care of by the time the hunt is over then you are justified in asking for a full or partial refund.

If an agency or oversight board regulates the guiding or outfitting business, you can file a complaint with them. In many states that regulate these businesses, the guides or outfitters must be bonded. If the regulators determine your complaint is legitimate, they can pressure the business to refund your money or give you a free hunt. If the business is found to be insolvent, then the bond may cover your refund. At the least, your complaint will be put in the guide's file and he may be put on probation. If complaints come in from other clients, the outfitter or guide may lose his license to operate.

If you want your money back simply because you did not get a buck or didn't even see a buck, you will be out of luck with most guides; success is dependent on too many things. Remember that if you do not follow the guide's plans, refuse to listen to his advice, or insist on doing things your way, you will have very little justification for complaining at the end of the hunt.

In our operation we got up at 4:00 A.M., had breakfast at 4:30 and were heading out of camp around 5:00, seldom later than 5:30 A.M. We rarely came back until well after dark. This made for long days and hunters would sometimes ask to sleep-in a little longer or head for camp a little early. I would gently remind them that the more time they put in hunting the better their chances were for a buck. I had two reasons for telling them this. First, it is true. Secondly, I wanted to let them know that if they chose to put in less than 100 percent effort they would have no room for complaining when the hunt was over.

Generally, guides are hard working, honest people who want to keep a good reputation. They do their best to provide successful hunts for their hunters. They want hunters to be satisfied and to return for several more hunts.

When you decide that a guided whitetail hunt is right for you, I hope this information will help you locate the right guide in a place where your chances are good for finding a trophy buck. If you are lucky, you will book with a guide who has an optimistic attitude to get you through the tough days. He will be patient when you are lagging behind and tolerant when you screw up. He will be genuinely thrilled for you when you kill that big buck. If you and your guide treat each other with respect and honesty, you will form a bond and friendship that will outlast the memories of the hunt.

CHAPTER 14

Last Hunt on the
State Piece

*I*daho *Whitetail Guides* was unique among Idaho's many guiding operations in a couple of ways. It was the only licensed guide service in the Lower Palouse drainage of Idaho and the only guide business hunting exclusively for whitetail deer. Most areas in Idaho had more than one outfitter and most other guiding businesses booked hunters for mixed species like elk, bear, deer, mountain lion, etc. Consequently, there was no interference from other guiding operations and we could really concentrate on whitetails.

Over the years we had the pleasure of guiding dozens of hunters and helping many of them find and kill big trophy bucks. Continually looking for new hunting areas was essential because conditions changed quickly and many areas that were good one year might be lost the next to logging, road building, no hunting signs, and sometimes to the fickle habits of whitetails when they decided they no longer liked a place. Carolyn and I spent a lot of time scouting for hunting spots and learning areas that were good and areas that were exceptionally good. This is the story of the last hunt in the very best of those exceptional areas in the years before it was lost to logging.

Our whitetail guiding area encompassed 460 square miles in the lower Panhandle of Idaho. This large guiding area contained dozens of small drainages ranging in size from less than 5,000 to over 20,000 acres.

These tributaries, all part of the Palouse River drainage, are identified by colorful and descriptive names like Hangman, Bluejacket, Last Chance, Poorman, and Headlong Creeks. Early gold miners, loggers, or fur trappers named the streams. Some names like Sypah (slow water), Wepah (bear), and Klawah (fast water) have their origins in the Chinook language used by trappers, fur traders, and Northwest Indian tribes.

The Palouse River drains several hundred square miles of forested mountains that are western foothills of the great Rocky Mountains. The river flows west across Idaho about where the Panhandle connects to the lower part of the state, enters the state of Washington, and eventually dumps into the Snake and Columbia River systems.

In this part of the country, parcels of land are identified by stream and river drainages, sometimes called watersheds. If you ask a logger here where he is working this week he will tell you "the Flat Creek drainage" or maybe just "Flat Creek." If you ask him to get more specific he might say "the State Piece in Flat Creek" or "the Potlatch Piece in Poorman Creek." What he means is the parcel of land owned by the state of Idaho that lies in the Flat Creek drainage or the section of land owned by the Potlatch Timber Company in Poorman Creek. Ranchers, miners, hunters, or anyone familiar with the area use the same terms.

One of the drainages within the Palouse River watershed that consistently produced big whitetail bucks in our early days of guiding was the Big Creek drainage. In appearance, the drainage is much like all the others in the Palouse. The stream and narrow valley bottom were mined for gold in the late 1800s and still have evidence of dredging, water diversions, and old mining campsites. The steep hillsides have undergone several waves of logging that have left huge whitepine stumps and old logging roads whose traces can still be seen.

The Big Creek drainage was first logged around the turn of the century, when loggers took out the western whitepine, leaving most of the other less valuable species. Since then, loggers have re-entered the drainage several times to harvest the cedar, red fir, and ponderosa pine depending on swings in the lumber market and the demands of homebuilders. As a result, the drainage is overlain with a maze of roads, skid trails, and logged over areas. The roads vary from unrecognizable, overgrown roads to recently constructed roads that are driveable only during the summer months. The logged areas include all ages of regeneration, from turn-of-the-century harvested areas where the only sign of logging is ancient whitepine stumps, to new, wide-open treeless clearcuts.

My favorite parcel of whitetail habitat in Big Creek was a 640 acre chunk of land owned by the state of Idaho that we called the "State Piece." The State Piece, in the late 1980s and early 1990s when I guided there, was somewhat unique in that it was one of the few remaining large parcels of land in Big Creek that had no recent roads or logging activity. Huge 200-year-old ponderosa pine, red fir, and cedar dominated the State Piece. These trees were so large and the canopies so dense that they supressed the small trees and kept the brushy undergrowth to a minimum.

This old forest provided great winter shelter for deer but had little for a food supply. However, there were plenty of adjacent, newly logged areas where deer could travel to for food. The State Piece was one of the last primeval whitetail habitats in this part of Idaho. It had changed little from the days when Lewis and Clark came over the Rockys in search of a route to the Pacific.

Carolyn and I discovered the State Piece in the spring of 1987, two years after we began our guiding business. We were on one of our favorite outings—hunting for shed antlers. We had driven up the Big Creek road through patches of leftover winter snow in the shady spots on the road. By the lack of vehicle tracks, it appeared we were the first to make it up as far as the State Piece. Our map told us this section of land was owned by the state of Idaho and managed by the Idaho Department of Lands.

That early April day we parked and headed into the timber on the north side of the narrow, rutted logging road. We hadn't gone more than 300 yards when a couple of things made us realize we were not in just another section of Idaho forest. The first was the size and age of the stand of trees and the second was a large whitetail shed. We were under a canopy of ponderosa pine and Douglas fir that towered more than 100 feet over our heads. Many of the trees were three feet in diameter with thick yellow bark indicating their ancient status among trees in the Big Creek drainage.

As I stood looking up at these old monarchs, Carolyn spotted the shed antler that would lead us to some of the best whitetail hunting in our entire 460 square mile guiding area. The antler had been shed a year or two earlier and was losing its red-brown color and starting to turn grayish green with some evidence of rodent chewing. There was no mistaking that this was from a grand old buck. It was a 5-point with a massive 26 inch main beam. The brow point was seven inches long, the first point beyond that was 11 inches, and the 3rd and 4th points had been chewed by rodents. The beam from the brow point down to the wide base was as thick as my wrist, rough and knurly with three or four odd points, each about one inch long. A conservative estimate would score this buck at about 170 B& C, maybe more.

We spent the rest of that day hiking through the State Piece, getting a feel for its size and shape and making some rough plans about how we might hunt it. With its steep terrain, deep draws, and sharp ridges, it wasn't an easy piece to move through. The dense canopy of those mature trees made it impossible to see distant landmarks that would normally help us keep our bearing. Even though it was a sunny day, we were traveling through a dark forest with only an occasional ray of filtered sunlight reaching the ground.

We were immediately impressed by the amount of buck sign. Every wet, mossy stream bottom had buck rubs and scrapes still evident from the previous November rut. Many of the rubbed trees were 4-6 inches in diameter and showed signs of being rubbed year after year by bucks with substantial antlers. Also, the ridges between these draws all had well used scrape lines, where bucks had been traveling the ridges. Game trails were apparent only in heavily used saddles, around edges of thick vegetation patches, and in stream bottoms.

As is typical for this part of Idaho, trails were short and difficult to follow for any distance since deer in these large, timbered tracts travel and feed at random as they move through the forests. In locations where terrain or cover forces them to follow the same routes, trails are evident but they often disappear as quickly as they appear. This took some getting used to for me, having come from Wisconsin. There I recall that deer generally feed in one location — agricultural croplands or acorn producing oak thickets — and bed in another. Their trails tend to be continuous, easy to follow, and consequently their habits more predictable.

We only explored a fraction of the extensive State Piece but we found three more whitetail sheds that day. Two were "fresh" sheds from the previous winter and were in perfect condition, with good brown color and no rodent damage. One of these was a large 4-point with long, heavy points and the other a less massive 5-point, maybe from a younger buck. Either of these sheds, given a matching side and modest 16-18 inch inside spread, would have scored in the upper 140s. The fourth antler we picked up that day was very old and had most of its points chewed off by rodents but what remained was enough to to tell us it was from a big buck. We had only spent 3-4 hours hiking and found antlers from four bucks that were all what I call "shootable bucks." This was definitely an area to learn more about to determine if it would be a suitable place for guiding hunters.

While guiding, it became apparent that each area we discovered had to be hunted differently. Most of our clients came from the East, Mid-west, or the South and were not accustomed to hunting large expanses of forest. As I have said before, they came with a wide range of experience, physical ability, and varying degrees of woods savvy. Some hunters could be given simple directions or a quickly drawn map and be fine stillhunting all day and returning to the truck at dark with little worry on my part. Others were very uncomfortable hunting alone in areas that were to them, large tracts of unknown wilderness. I guided hunters who absolutely did not want to be left alone or who would not venture beyond sight of the pickup truck.

Areas with old logging roads, well-defined ridges, or simple stream patterns that could be followed were easiest for hunters to stillhunt. If I were guiding a hunter who was experienced and confident I could send him alone to stillhunt these areas with good results. Other areas with no definite patterns of ridges, streams, or roads, or where vegetation was very thick, were difficult to hunt without getting lost. As a rule, I had my hunters use treestands in those difficult areas.

The State Piece was one of those places that proved to be very difficult to stillhunt. The timbered hillsides were steep and cut with sharp ravines. The terrain was so broken with ridges and the big trees so dense that a hunter could not see more than 100 yards. The hunters who were game to try it usually only got to see fleeting tails as deer dropped out of sight over the next ridge. In spite of the difficulties it posed, the State Piece was so torn-up with buck sign and produced such large shed antlers every spring that we kept returning to it looking for ways that hunters could hunt it. In 1988, I finally put in the effort to really scout it for tree and ground stand locations and we started killing good bucks.

The Palouse River drainage, indeed all of north Idaho whitetail country, is not known for its high deer densities. Game surveys by the Idaho Department of Fish and Game put the numbers at between 10 and 15 deer per square mile of whitetail habitat. This is a low whitetail density compared to areas in midwestern, New England, and southern states where densities commonly reach more than 30 deer per square mile. The number of deer in the State Piece appeared to be no greater than in other drainages in our guiding area but it was outstanding in producing big bucks.

For some reason only known to the deer, these ancient forests on the State Piece were prime rutting areas. The ridges and creek bottoms showed evidence of scrape routes and rub trees used year after year. By early October I would start seeing signs of scrapes and by November the mature forest was alive with signs of the fall rut. The years from 1989 to 1997 were the heyday for our guiding business on the State Piece. Over those years, our hunters took several bucks from the drainage, which scored from 140 to 150 B&C points, the biggest being a non-typical killed in 1989 that scored 196.

However, forests that produce big bucks can also produce valuable timber and in good timber production land the inevitable is sure to happen. Logging companies on private land, the U.S. Forest Service on national forest land, and the Idaho Department of Lands on state land began to log those magnificent chunks of near pristine forest in Big Creek at an alarming rate. Log prices were high and by the end of those glorious hunting years much of what was often referred to as "old growth" in the drainage had been logged.

I had started making my usual preparations for the 1997 fall hunt earlier that summer. As I scouted my favorite areas, my heart began to sink as I discovered that logging during the year had reduced the mature forests even further. The State Piece had not been logged, but foresters cruising timber that summer had marked trees in this section indicating it was destined to be logged. They had spray-painted a message on the big tamarack where I had one of my stands with the message "THIS TREE WILL BE CUT." My feelings were of disappointment and sadness but I also felt somewhat appreciative that they had been considerate enough to let me know that the inevitable was coming. They wouldn't be starting this harvest until later that fall. We might have a chance for one last hunt on the State Piece.

I had booked Bob and Ralph, two hunters from the Adirondak region of New York State who were coming for the last week of the season. This was Bob's third year to hunt with us. Of the hunters I had guided, Bob was near the top of my "favorite hunters" list. In his late 50s, Bob was full of enthusiasm and had a genuine love for and curiosity about everything outdoors. Bob was over six feet tall, with dark hair and a year-around tanned look he got from his Native American heritage. Bob would joke that it was his Mohican blood that made him such a great hunter, but it also gave him rugged good looks that could have landed him the lead role of "Chief" in a James Fenimore Cooper movie.

Each of the first two years Bob hunted with us, he killed

good bucks. However, he was one of those rare hunters who got more out of hunting than just getting a trophy whitetail. He was an extremely observant hunter and a day never went by without him seeing game. Even if it were only a coyote trotting past his stand or a moose feeding on a far hillside, Bob would be bubbling with excitement. He was a great storyteller and loved entertaining the rest of us at the dinner table with descriptions of what he had seen and where he had hunted that day. Never complaining, always enthusiastic, and quick to adapt to any new hunting situation, Bob was a joy to guide.

He had come alone on his first two hunts but had invited his hunting partner, Ralph, to join him on this 1997 hunt. Ralph, who was about ten years younger than Bob, had a more reserved demeanor. But he was an equal to Bob in his hunting ability and his woodsmanship. Together they made one of the greatest hunting pairs I ever guided.

Bob had told me before the hunt started that more than anything, he wanted Ralph to get a good buck. He emphasized that I should put Ralph in the best stands or send him on the best stillhunts whenever there was a choice. This was typical of Bob's generous and unselfish nature.

Bob had hunted the State Piece on his previous hunts and killed his last Idaho buck there. He was always in awe of the huge timber and untouched beauty in the Piece. In a phone conversation during the summer of 1997, I had reluctantly let him know that the Piece was scheduled to be logged, that trees were marked with paint and roads were laid out with ribbon and stakes. I had talked with state foresters, who indicated logging could start anytime that fall.

So, it was not surprising when Bob requested that we hunt there as much as possible this third-year if we could beat the logging. I had put up treestands in four of the best buck areas on the Piece. I knew how much it would mean to Bob if he and Ralph could be the last to hunt it.

The day before these New York boys were to arrive in Idaho, I drove to the State Piece and found that, so far, luck was with us — logging hadn't started.

After their arrival, the three of us decided that we would concentrate the entire week on the Piece. This was not my usual approach, since I normally moved hunters to new areas every couple of days. However, Bob knew the Piece well and Ralph was game to go with whatever we thought. Logging could start any day and we had to hunt while we could.

Monday, the first day out, I was hiking them in to treestands on an old game trail. We paused to catch our breaths and to cool down so they would not be too hot for sitting. The ground had about three inches of snow and the faint light of dawn made seeing just possible. As we stood silently in these early pre-dawn minutes, we could make out the movements of two deer about 50 yards away and slightly below us in a small opening in the timber. Ralph eased his rifle up to check if he could see better through his scope. These deer were not feeding, passing through, or standing looking at us—they had not seen us. Instead, they were acting like a buck and doe in courtship mode. The smaller of the two would make a quick dash for a few feet, then whirl and dash back. The larger deer only turned to watch the antics of the other.

Looking over Ralph's shoulder I whispered, "Looks like a buck and doe rutting." He slowly nodded his head in agreement, not taking his eyes off his scope.

After a few moments, the doe made another squirrely dash that took her across the opening and disappeared into the heavy timber. The big deer lowered his head and started following. As he crossed the glade I could see his silhouette against the snow-covered background. I could see lots of antlers, though I could not make out detail. I didn't know how well Ralph could see through the scope and I had no idea if he was planning to shoot.

Before the big buck entered the dense timber I stopped him by making a low grunt with my mouth and whispered, "Looks like a good one" in Ralph's ear. Instantly, the .35 Whelen boomed and the muzzle flash lit up the morning darkness. The buck dove into the timber then just as quickly bounded back into the glade and ran straight toward us. At about 30 feet he turned to our right and was gone into the dark timber. The three of us stood there dumbfounded. We had just seen a dandy buck, and had also witnessed Ralph's clean miss!

On Tuesday, day two of the hunt, we again headed into the State Piece. As we passed the spot where Ralph missed, we stopped for a moment like three coyotes pausing to remember a grouse that had gotten away. The plan for the day was for the hunters to sit in their stands until mid-morning. I was to hike farther up the drainage, hunker down until about 10:00 A.M., then make a slow meandering push back to Bob and Ralph in their stands.

It was 10:00 and I had just started moving toward the hunters when I heard a shot. I continued my deer drive and eventually came to Ralph's stand. He hadn't shot so we headed for Bob's stand about 300 yards farther up the ridge. There he stood waiting at his stand with a big grin and obviously a story to tell.

At about 9:30 he had seen a doe heading in my direction, but she was 100 yards up the ridge from Bob's stand where a shot

Bob from New York enjoyed every aspect of whitetail hunting—just being in the woods made him happy. This 8-pointer was the last buck he killed.

would be difficult. Bob said he had a feeling that a buck might eventually follow her so he climbed down and moved closer to the trail where the doe had traveled. At about 10:00 he heard a deer coming toward him. It was a buck that was grunting and traveling with his nose to the ground in the direction the doe had gone. Bob made a clean kill at 30 yards with his Sako .243.

The buck was not large, but had a beautifully symmetrical 8-point rack. Bob told us he just couldn't pass this one up considering how he was feeling. He hadn't mentioned it before but now he told Ralph and me that since he got to Idaho he had not been feeling up to par. The hills seemed higher and steeper than ever and he was often short of breath. I didn't think much of it at the time, but it was an early warning of what lay ahead for Bob.

Ralph and I continued to hunt the State Piece throughout the week. Bob stayed close to camp, skinned and butchered his buck and generally enjoyed himself.

On Friday the three of us went out together. Ralph, who by now knew his way around, went into a treestand on a high ridge on the State Piece. Just before noon I went in to get him. We did some rattling in a couple locations on our way out but got no response.

Our 6-inches of snow had frozen and made stillhunting next to impossible. Ralph's best bet was to go back to the ridge treestand after lunch and stay until dark. I told Ralph I would pick him up at the trailhead at dark and I took Bob back to camp.

Time was running out for Ralph, and Bob was beginning to worry that his friend would not get a buck. He was more concerned about it than Ralph was. At mid-afternoon on that last Friday in November, Ralph's luck changed.

Ralph's treestand was about 50 yards down the west side of the ridge and 15-feet off the ground in a clump of ponderosa pines. This put him at eye-level with the ridge top and he could also see downhill for 75 yards. We had used this stand location for many years and had taken 3-4 bucks from it, but none that scored more than 140 points.

At 3:15 that afternoon, Ralph could hear the unmistakable sound of a deer walking in the crusty snow and moving in from the south. It sounded as though it was coming at about his level on the hillside. Ralph shouldered his rifle and got ready. When the buck appeared it was about 40 yards away and coming straight on.

Ralph later told us, "I couldn't believe my eyes. I had never seen such a big buck or such massive antlers. The rack was inches past his ears and the points were long and thick. The buck turned to angle up the slope and I could see the long, heavy left beam with points that looked like candles on one of those fancy candelabras."

Ralph made a good forward lung shot catching part of the shoulder. The big 250 grain bullet from his .35 Whelen put the buck down in its tracks.

The real highlight of the day was when Ralph and I drove into camp with this great buck. Bob ran out to greet us, threw his arms around Ralph and gave him a bear hug. Being a true friend, it was obvious that Bob was happier for Ralph than if he had killed the buck himself.

That big 5X6 buck had a gross score of 161 B&C points, making it one of the best bucks any of our hunters killed. It was late in the rut and this old boy was run down and in poor condition but he still field dressed at 185 pounds.

This was a fitting way to end hunting on the State Piece. That winter, the entire section was harvested. I have a mixture of feelings when I look back on my guiding days in the Piece. I feel extremely fortunate to have had a chance to hunt in a place nearly untouched by man. At the same time I feel profoundly sad to have seen the last hunt in that magnificent forest.

Bob never hunted the State Piece again. He booked a hunt for the following year and three weeks before the hunt was to start he died from heart failure. In a way, I'm glad he didn't come. I know he would have wanted to at least take a look at his favorite hunting spot. However, it was unrecognizable. Only the stumps remained where the giant pines and firs stood over the buck scrapes and game trails. The quiet, moss covered trails were replaced by muddy roads and skid trails.

I have come to accept that good hunting spots are like other good things in our lives—they don't always stay that way. Like the shine of a new pickup, the bluing on a good rifle, or the keen nose of a bird dog, a great whitetail hunting spot eventually must go. I lost many hunting areas during my guiding years but the State Piece held such great memories for me it was the toughest to let go of.

Hopefully, there will come a day when someone in a future generation will be able to hunt this area as we did; when its trees are again three feet in diameter and 100 feet tall and its floor is carpeted with quiet, green moss and tiny cascading streams that run so clear that you won't hesitate to bend down and take a drink. When you cannot see the sky through the immense canopy cathedral or feel the wind when it blows strong everywhere else. Where the varied thrush, the pine squirrel, the martin, and the snowshoe hare; the multitude of plants, fungi, mosses, and lichens; and the big creatures like the moose, elk, whitetail deer and black bear once again live like they had lived for eons.

This big 5X6 whitetail was the last buck taken from the State Piece before it was logged. Ralph (right) shot it at 35 yards while treestand hunting.

CHAPTER 15

Venison Done Right

I honestly feel there is no finer meat than venison if it has been well taken care of and correctly prepared. However, I didn't always feel this way. I grew up eating lots of deer meat, but, I didn't like it all that much. I would have listed it along with spinach, rutabagas, and cauliflower—edible but certainly not great. I am convinced now that the reason I didn't like it was because we didn't take proper care of it or cook it right.

In Wisconsin, we would kill our deer the last week of November. They would hang from two to four weeks with the hides on, in what we called the "machine shed" on our farm. During that aging process the weather in Wisconsin was generally cold, so they were frozen at least part of the time.

We would then drag them into the basement of our big farmhouse and let them thaw for a day or two. Dad would skin them and start butchering. He was a "waste-not, want-not" man and believed in using every ounce of deer meat.

In those days, boning-out was unheard of, at least in our family. My older brother, Dennis, and I would help by holding the big semi-frozen chunks while Dad would use a hand meat saw. He would cut through meat and bone at the same time. His cuts always looked great, like you would see in a butcher shop. I could tell T-bone from club steaks and sirloin from rump roasts. What didn't make steaks was cut into roasts. He would even cut all the ribs into sections for rib roasts.

These cuts would only get wrapped in freezer paper that

had wax on one side. We didn't use clear plastic wrap; it may not have been invented yet. These packages would go into the freezer and make up a large part of our yearly meat supply.

Looking back on those days, I know why I was only mildly keen on the stuff. It had been left hanging too long with the hide on in varying temperatures, probably freezing and thawing, and poorly wrapped, with bone and fat left with the meat. My mother was then stuck with the difficult job of trying to make good table fare out of poor meat.

Bless her heart, she tried her best but like most farm women in those days, she cooked venison (or any meat for that matter) until it was very well done. She would roll the steaks in salted flour and fry them in grease. She would fry them until the only flavor and moisture left were of the salt and grease.

The roasts were no better. Mom would oven-roast those big chunks of meat until they had no sign of pink meat and were done through and through. By then, they were so dry and flavorless we could hardly swallow a piece without choking.

The ribs were the worst of all. Believe me, you have not lived until you have eaten venison ribs roasted in the oven until well done. We called them "tallowy," a term most hunters these days are unfamiliar with. The fat of a deer has a higher melting point than beef. When it cools just a little (about cool enough to put in your mouth) it solidifies into tallow. Tallow from those venison ribs would solidify on our plates, forks, and on our lips and the roof of our mouths.

To minimize the tallow from a rib roast, Mom would preheat our plates in her cookstove oven. We would eat fast before the ribs and the plates cooled. That seemed to help, but tallow is nasty stuff and by the time we were done with a meal everything tasted like deer fat and it was all over like candle wax.

Many of the hunters we guided must have grown up eating venison like I did. If they did, I can understand why so many of them were not the least bit interested in the meat. They viewed the meat as an inconvenience. By law, they could not waste it, so it became a burden. I was often stuck trying to give the meat away after the hunters went home with their capes and antlers.

It was rare to guide a hunter who was actually happy to have deer meat, anxious to take it home, and who knew how (or had a wife who knew how) to prepare it for the table.

This is a shame because venison can be delicious. I have come to that conclusion after changing the way I handle the carcass, and how I cut and wrap the meat. My wife, Carolyn, has learned to cook it in ways that Mom never dreamed of.

I am now a firm believer in cooling a deer quickly once it is dead. Getting the hide off is the best first move you can make in cooling the meat. After it has cooled and stiffened it can be cut and wrapped.

I do not skin in the field since it is difficult to keep the meat clean but I skin as soon as I get the deer home. Then I cut it up and wrap it within a day or two depending on the temperature outside. I no longer see any value in "aging" venison.

If a deer has been gut shot, it should be washed out with cold water. You can hang it and use a garden hose or throw buckets of clean water into the body cavity.

Carolyn Skille and a yearling buck she shot with her single shot .22 Hornet.
This deer is a dedicated meat hunter's dream-come-true.

A friend of mine runs a local butcher shop and cuts up dozens of deer each year. He tells me that many hunters who bring deer to him are reluctant to get the carcass wet for fear it will ruin the meat. He views this as an old wives' tale that seems to be perpetuated among hunters. If the meat is dirty from being gut shot, has a lot of hair on it or is just dirty from being handled it should be washed. However, it is important to let the excess water drain off and the meat allowed to air out and cool down.

If you cut and wrap your own deer, it is easiest to bone out the meat and remove as much fat as possible. Bone just takes up space and fat spoils fast and can taint entire packages. Meat should be wrapped in clear plastic-wrap, then wrapped in butcher paper. Be careful to get as much air out of the package as possible so the meat does not freezer burn. Freezer burning occurs when cold air gets into the package and actually freeze-dries the outer layers of meat, leaving a bad flavor.

If you read books on whitetail hunting you will notice that many writers take you right up through field dressing the deer and caping the trophy head, then stop. My guess is that writers know that is where the interest of many hunters ends. To have good eating venison, it is the hunter's responsibility to follow the process all the way to the table. If you just leave it up to the cook and hope for the best then all the care that went into the meat can be wasted. Using the right recipes is critical.

Carolyn did all the cooking for our hunters and guides. Her kitchen was the favorite place for hunters to congregate, so much so that often she would have to chase them out so she had room to cook. Since this was a deer camp we felt it was appropriate to serve venison at least a couple times during each hunter's stay. There was usually a good supply of fresh venison since most hunters were proud to provide meat from their deer.

Over the years Carolyn tried several recipes and ways of preparing venison. The hunters and guides were good testing grounds and she was able to get honest feedback about which recipes were keepers and which to toss.

Consequently, the recipes described here are the best-of-the-best and are not here to just fill the pages of this book. We se-

One of Carolyn Skille's 4:30 A.M. hunter's breakfasts.

lected them because they proved themselves over 14 years in our hunting camp. We often had hunters let us know outright that they could not stand deer meat. Most of them changed their minds after trying these dishes. Many asked for the recipes so their wives could make the same meals at home.

If you are already a venison lover, these recipes will give you a variety of ways for preparing it. If you are a reluctant venison eater or have given up on it altogether, Carolyn and I hope you will give these recipes a try. You might just change your mind and begin to love the meat as much as the hunting.

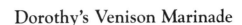

Dorothy's Venison Marinade

Carolyn considers this the very best venison recipe. It came from Dorothy, the wife of Roy, one of our hunters. Carolyn made venison using this one at least once during every week of our guided hunts. It was by far the favorite among all the recipes. If a deer hunter or anyone else doesn't like this one, they qualify as a true vegetarian.

Ingredients:

   2 pounds venison steak
   1/3 cup soy sauce
   1 tablespoon minced onion
   2 crushed garlic cloves
   1/2 teaspoon ginger
   2 bay leaves
   1/3 cup vegetable oil
   1 tablespoon sugar

Cut the meat into serving pieces (even tiny steaks work fine) and place in a covered glass or plastic pan. Combine ingredients and pour over venison. Cover and marinate over night at a minimum (3-4 days in refrigerator is good for tougher cuts). Turn the meat once a day. Broil in the oven on a foil covered cookie sheet for five minutes on each side—do not over-cook. Baste with marinade during cooking if you like.

Venison Swiss Steak

This is another easy one and can be made with tough cuts of venison. It cooks for 2-3 hours and makes the toughest cut of meat tender enough to cut with a fork.

Ingredients:
    2 pounds venison round steaks
    2 cans Italian stewed tomatoes
    2 medium onions
    1/2 cup white flour
    1 teaspoon salt
    1/4 teaspoon black pepper

Pound seasoned flour (flour, salt, and pepper) into both sides of steaks. Sauté two sliced onions in a greased electric fry pan. Remove the onions and brown the steaks on both sides. Top with the browned onions and add two cans of Italian stewed tomatoes. Cover and cook slowly until tender, about 2-1/2 to 3 hours. Serve with French Bread Monterey*.

John's Venison Pepper Steak

This is a favorite from my good friend and hunting partner. John is always looking for a big buck but he loves venison so much he has a hard time passing up the small, good-eating ones! This one works great whether they are old and tough or young and tender.

Ingredients:

    3 pounds venison steak
    2 red bell peppers, halved and slices
    2 onions, halved and slices
    2 cans Italian stewed tomatoes
    1 small can sliced mushrooms (or sliced fresh)
    1 tablespoon chopped garlic (or to taste)
    1 tablespoon Worcestershire sauce
    1 cup Marsala wine
    1 ounce olive oil
    blackened pepper
    peanut or olive oil

Season the steaks with blackened pepper and brown them in peanut or olive oil (if you use olive oil, keep the heat no higher than medium). Cover the bottom of a large baking dish with steaks and layer on ingredients except the Worcestershire, wine, and olive oil. Repeat the layering. Add Marsala, Worcestershire, and olive oil. Cover and bake at 325 degrees for about 3-1/2 hours or until meat is falling-apart tender.

Ralph's Special Venison

Ralph and Bob from the northern part of New York State hunted with us. Each time one of them killed a buck, they celebrated by using this recipe to prepare a meal for us. Carolyn got to sit back and relax on those days. It became one of our favorite venison recipes.

Ingredients:

    1-1/2 pound venison steaks
    1/2 cup cooking oil
    1 tablespoon minced garlic
    1 teaspoon rosemary
    1/2 cup red wine vinegar

Marinate the venison in the oil, garlic, and rosemary mixture for one hour. Pre-heat a frying pan to hot and quickly brown both sides of the steaks. Add one-half cup water and one-half cup red wine vinegar, cover and simmer until most of the liquid is gone, about 1-1/2 to 2 hours.

Venison Meal-In-Itself

Ingredients:

1 pound ground venison
1/2 cup spaghetti noodles
1/4 cup dry sherry
1 cup chopped onion
2 cups thinly sliced carrots
2 cups chopped celery
1 can (15 ounces) tomato sauce
2 teaspoons diced basil
6 beef bullion cubes
1 bay leaf

Brown the venison in a lightly greased deep frying pan. Add the chopped onion and cook until translucent. Stir in seven cups of water and add all the ingredients except the noodles and dry sherry. Cook for one hour. Break the spaghetti noodles, add to the mixture, and cook 30 minutes longer. Before serving remove the bay leaf and add the dry sherry.

Venison Meat Balls

A good one if you think your deer might be a little strong or gamy. This will help to cover any wild flavor.

Ingredients:

2 pounds ground venison
2 eggs, lightly beaten
1 cup (4 ounces) shredded Mozzarella cheese
1/2 cup dry breadcrumbs
1/4 cup finely chopped onions
2 tablespoons grated Parmesan cheese
1 tablespoon ketchup
2 teaspoons Worcestershire sauce
1 teaspoon Italian seasoning
1 teaspoon dried basil
1 teaspoon salt
1/4 teaspoon black pepper

Combine all ingredients in a bowl and mix well. Shape mixture into 1-inch diameter balls. Place meatballs on a rack in a shallow roasting pan and bake at 350 degrees for 10-15 minutes. Remove and drain off the grease. Use these meatballs to make spaghetti by adding to homemade or store purchased canned spaghetti sauce. Serve spaghetti with a green salad and French Bread Monterey*.

* French Bread Monterey

This easy to make French bread was always a hit with any of the venison recipes, especially venison Swiss steak and venison meatballs and spaghetti.

Ingredients:
    1 large loaf French bread
    1 cup Miracle Whip salad dressing
    1/2 cup grated Parmesan cheese
    1/2 cup finely chopped onion
    1/2 teaspoon Worcestershire sauce

Cut the loaf of bread into 1-inch slices, wrap in foil, and place in the oven to warm. Meanwhile, mix the other ingredients to be used as a bread topping. Remove warmed bread from oven and spread one side of each slice with the mixture. Sprinkle lightly with paprika and broil until bubbly.

Acknowledgements

I am indebted to the following people who made our guiding business successful and the writing of this book possible:

To all those whitetail hunters who took their chances on booking hunts with me. They taught me much about hunting and guiding—without them I would have had nothing to write about.

To my guides, Kelly Phillips, Donny Ball, Lonie Austin, and Brian Painter who I could count on to look after hunters and bring them back each day safe and sound—it was tougher work than anyone can imagine.

To my wife, Carolyn, who helped in every way with the guiding business. She was the one who could turn the wet, tired, grumbly hunters and guides into happy souls with her great meals and positive, laughing ways.

To Rick Stowell, Andy Porter, and Carolyn Skille who edited my writing and helped to make sense out of it.

To the late Aileen Reynolds Hall, our local artist, who made the trophy buck pencil drawing used on the first pages of each chapter throughout the book.

To hunters, guides, and everyone who supplied photographs for this book.

I give all of you my sincere thanks.

Jack Skille

About the Author:

Jack Skille grew up in northern Wisconsin's great whitetail country. Born into a family of guides and hunters, he started guiding while still in high school. In 1985, he started *Idaho Whitetail Guides*, an outfitting business in the Panhandle region of Idaho. For 14 years he guided hunters from all over the United States into some of the best trophy buck hunting found anywhere. He is a dedicated whitetail hunter and student of wildlife with M.S. and Ph.D. degrees in wildlife biology. Jack Skille and his wife, Carolyn, live in northern Idaho where he continues to pursue big bucks with rifle and bow.